50 things you really need to know

FANTASTIC FIRST-TIME FATHER

Tim Mungeam

Quercus

Contents

Introduction

On the whole, men aren't huge readers of parenting books, but however you arrived here, I'm glad you did. Even though you may not have actually made the purchase, the fact that you're reading this now means a lot. It means you're ready to get stuck into being a great dad.

From day one, my intention in writing this book was to put together a practical, issues-focused companion to early fatherhood, which also looked at the personal, emotional adjustment that every man needs to make as he gets to grips with becoming a dad. It doesn't need to be read in order, so please feel free to dip in and out. As you do, I hope that you'll soon find yourself moving beyond the (all important) 'which wet wipe is better?' question and find yourself thinking about your whole approach to the messy but wonderful world that is fatherhood. Becoming a brand new, first-time dad is an uncharted journey, but it's also a chance to make your particular mark.

The book takes the view that being a dad is more of an art than a science – finding your own interpretation of what fatherhood means for you and your son, or you and your daughter. Unfortunately there's no sure-fire way to raise a perfect and happy child. I'd love to be able to tell you that success is guaranteed but it's not. It's life's greatest adventure, but it's life's greatest experiment too. There's a lot of fun to be had but you'll need to be prepared for a few explosions and the finished product may not turn out the way you expected.

However it goes for you, never forget this: fantastic first-time fathers know that, amidst the chaos and unpredictability, the secret of really successful fatherhood is simply sticking at it.

Tim Mungeam

(1) Can I do this?

Becoming a dad is the start of a thrilling journey. However, it may not feel like that when you first hear the news – shock, panic and fear are common reactions to all major adjustments, and this may be the biggest life adjustment that you'll ever be asked to undertake.

Me? A dad?

From the moment your partner, wife or girlfriend told you that she was expecting, the likelihood is that you will have found yourself battling a range of conflicting emotions: delight, fear, excitement, anxiety, confidence and insecurity. It may feel as though your every action and decision now carries a new significance, with implications not only for you but for two other people. The buck stops here. In an instant, life has changed and at times the responsibility can feel overwhelming. Questions like 'Am I ready?', 'Am I mature enough?' and 'Can we afford it?' will be making regular appearances in the forefront of your mind.

All these questions are perfectly normal – beginning to ask yourself these kinds of things is an important stage in preparing yourself for fatherhood. But the truthful answer to most of them is probably 'no'. Put simply, no-one can ever be completely prepared because parenthood first time around is a journey into the unknown.

Your legacy

Becoming a dad is an incredible privilege and you'll soon realize that fatherhood is the most important job you'll ever have. Forget the dreams of businessmen and politicians – fatherhood guarantees that you'll leave a flesh-and-blood legacy: your child. If that sounds daunting, you're probably in the right place, psychologically speaking. The actor Ed Asner summed up the essence of early parenthood perfectly when he jokingly described it as 'part joy, part guerrilla warfare'. The life of a new dad is punctuated with many 'top of the world' moments but these will be accompanied by a fair share of moments where you ask yourself, 'How did I get myself into this?'. But the truth is, you only need to spend a little time in the presence of a loving father and his daughter or son to see that the rewards of fatherhood are well worth the effort.

Keep calm and carry on

The early days of discovering that you're going to be a dad can be stressful but try not to get overwhelmed. The four 'Rs' of fatherhood are handy to remember at this stage:

- Resolve to be an informed, committed, involved dad from day one, even if you're quaking in your boots.
- Relax – you can't anticipate everything, so don't even start thinking about how you can plan everything out onto an Excel spreadsheet.
- Reach out to your partner – she is probably just as anxious as you, even if she seems completely elated. This is a big step for both of you.
- Remember that a mixture of emotions is perfectly natural. If you have any ideas about how the 'perfect dad' wouldn't feel anything but joy, take a quick peek at page 12. Humans are complicated and so are their reactions and emotions.

Six billion plus one

It's estimated that worldwide, 252 children are born every minute. That's four brand new babies a second. You may think that you've had a hectic 24 hours, but since this time yesterday the global population has increased by a hefty 362,880 people. In the time it took you to read this paragraph, the lungs of two football teams' worth of children have taken their first breaths. It's a mind-boggling statistic.

On the other hand, the fact that a third of a million babies have been born since yesterday and a further six billion people have successfully negotiated their way into the global village already probably makes zero difference to the way you feel at the moment. Because now it's your turn: your baby, your partner's pregnancy and your journey into fatherhood. This whole child-rearing thing looks very different when it's up close and personal. But remember this: despite the alarming nature of the task, many, many other dads have done it. Look around you. If those guys can do it, you can too.

In just 24 hours, around 363,000 babies are born – that's 252 a minute

Don't try to be John Wayne

As you go through this major life-adjustment, you'll probably find yourself evaluating your goals and priorities, and this is important, because it will help you define your role as dad for yourself, rather than accepting some media or big-screen version. What are the big things that are important to you in your life? What aspects of your personality and character would you like your child to inherit? More importantly, what would you prefer they didn't? What kind of role would you like to play in this little person's life?

Becoming a dad will force you to really examine who you are, and how you came to be that person. We're talking about examining bedrock beliefs here, so no wonder it feels alarming. While you might be tempted to put on a strong, silent front, mentally retreating to a cave and pretending nothing much is happening, this isn't the way to play it. Successful parenthood depends upon genuine

> Wow! @Sophie's just told me we're having a baby. Delighted and excited. Need to sit down. #responsibilitybites

communication. Many men believe that it's their job to protect their partner and, during pregnancy, this can translate into a wish not to 'bother her' with their own concerns. However, a moment's reflection shows this to be faulty thinking. Your partner needs to know that you're as involved as she is, and by talking about your thoughts and concerns, she'll realize that both of you are in this together. She'll feel more confident that you understand what she's going through. And by acknowledging your feelings, you'll find out just how normal they really are.

Condensed idea
Becoming a dad is a fantastic but life-changing experience

Evidence shows that involved, informed dads have a vital role to play in helping their sons and daughters grow up to be rounded, secure and happy individuals. Kids can't rely on mums alone.

Dads are important

Most parenting books are aimed at mums and focus on the health and wellbeing of the woman and her baby through pregnancy and birth. This seems about right, given that mums are at the sharp end of early parenthood. As someone who can just about handle a dose of 'man flu', I can't begin to imagine how I would negotiate morning sickness,

let alone experience agonizing contractions and hours of labour. The flipside of this focus on maternity, however, is that we can lose sight of the crucial contribution that dads can make too.

Every dad – just like every mum – matters. Research shows that informed, open-minded and ever-ready-to-learn dads can make all the difference to how good their children feel about themselves. Children with supportive dads are, for example, better at forming friendships. They exhibit fewer behavioural problems and tend to do better at school. Evidence suggests that the influence of a loving, 'get stuck in' dad from an early age reaps rewards later in life too, helping a child grow into a secure, confident adult, who is better at building and retaining relationships.

Male and female brains

The importance of fathers to their children is becoming better understood. Men and women are certainly equal, but they are not identical – studies are constantly advancing our understanding of how male and female brains work, and pointing up the differences. Neuroscientists and psychologists who have studied gender and brain difference talk about 'male' and 'female' brains to emphasize two extremes of a spectrum. On the extreme 'male' end of the spectrum, the skills involved in systematizing and categorizing are exceptional, while at the 'female' extreme, the skills involved in understanding and caring for other people

> I seem to have mislaid my fatherhood instruction manual. I think it might be with the car keys (wherever they are...). #missionimpossible?

are paramount. However, real men and women fall somewhere along this line, with some men cultivating great emotional intelligence skills, and some women being brilliant at systems and logical compartmentalizing.

What does all this mean for parenting? One thing it means – if you tend towards the extreme male end of the spectrum – is that you probably want to skip the advice in the last chapter that suggests talking openly and honestly to your partner, and sharing your feelings. But it also means that you're likely to be good at looking at impending parenthood in a different way to your partner.

Take a look around your local town. You'll probably notice that mums often walk with babies in a sling holding the baby's face pointing inwards, towards them, while dads favour pointing the baby's face outwards, towards the world. While your partner is thinking about your child's internal world, it's likely that you'll have more of an eye on his external world – noticing the potential harms that might befall him, and the great opportunities within his grasp.

Dad facts

The role a father plays in his children's day-to-day life has changed dramatically over the years.

- British fathers' care of infants and young children rose by 800 per cent between 1975 and 1997, from 15 minutes to two hours on an average working day.
- In the UK, dads in two-parent families do an average of 25 per cent of the childcare-related activities during the week and 30 per cent at weekends.
- The pace of change is increasing. Between 2002 and 2005, the percentage of new fathers in the UK who chose flexible working hours to spend more time with their babies, rose from 11 per cent to 31 per cent.
- In the USA, married fathers more than doubled the time spent exclusively on childcare activities from 2.6 hours per week in 1965 to 6.5 hours in 2000.
- Australian fathers' care of children has also risen dramatically, especially the time spent in sole charge of children at home.

Risk ready

Psychological research has shown that men are more likely to take risks than women. There are several reasons for this, but perhaps the main one is that the area of the brain that weighs up risks and possible outcomes (the frontal lobes) is guarded by a filtering system called the Reticular Activating System (RAS). Simply put, this filter prevents your brain from suffering 'data overload', by helping you to choose what to pay attention to and what to ignore. In the female brain, it lets through lots of information, so women see and assess risk clearly. In the male brain, however, the filter lets through much less information. It takes much more for the male brain to 'wake up' to risk, with the result that we're likely to drive faster and jump higher off diving boards. This was probably very handy when we were engaged in the risky business of hunting bison and living in caves. Meanwhile, the mums were collecting vegetation to eat, lighting fires, making clothes, and running camps, all while watching that the kids didn't get eaten by a passing fearsome wild animal.

If you want to see this risk-taking in action, watch a dad with his child. Parenting expert Professor Ross D. Parke suggests that the dad will, most likely, be picking her up, lifting her high into the air and throwing his head back so that they are looking into each other's faces. As she laughs, he'll lower her back down, give her a shake and a tickle, and hoist her into the air again. Later on, mum might sit her daughter on her lap, talking and singing, while the baby watches, transfixed and calm.

Dads are not second-class mums

Dispel the notion that one of you will be a 'primary' and the other a 'secondary' carer. Challenge prejudice when you encounter it, but also notice when you occasionally fall into the extremes of the 'male' brain pattern. Your mission is to model your best version of what positive masculinity looks like. It will mean showing your son or daughter how a good man should be. Oh, and one more thing about the male brain? It not only takes longer to 'wake up' – it also gets bored more quickly and goes 'back to sleep' faster than the female one. Which means at night, you'll be slower to wake and faster to get back to sleep than your partner. She'll envy you that one, believe me.

Condensed idea
Play to your strengths and work on your weaknesses

3 No one's perfect

Despite the impression we sometimes get from magazines and TV commercials, there is no such thing as the perfect parent. But you can be a proud, successful (and imperfect) first-time father. Keep talking to your partner and be ready to learn from your mistakes.

The myth of the 'Perfect Dad'

A few years ago my wife and I were invited round for a meal by some old friends. Over the previous year and a half we had noticed some subtle shifts in our relationship with them, following the arrival of their energetic baby boy. Now, when they suggested meeting up, they no longer meant a night out on the town. It meant a midday or early evening meal, usually at our house (the latter running strictly from 6.00–9.00 p.m.).

This particular evening, however, we were treated to new, fascinating insights into family life as the baby was present. We watched, entranced, as our hosts' young son took command, masterfully controlling the behaviour of his still-novice mum and dad.

Our friends uncomplainingly and repeatedly picked up food from the floor wherever their little darling threw it. They patiently negotiated every morsel of lovingly prepared food into his mouth. They displayed weak smiles when he threw the mother of all tantrums, meekly 'rewarding' his behaviour by plonking him down in front his favourite TV show for a while just to shut him up. My wife and I exchanged secret knowing glances. She knew what I was thinking. There was no way I would ever let our kids behave this way. At our house we, the parents, would be firmly in control.

There was of course only one problem with my steely determination. I wasn't a dad myself yet. In fact, it would be some years before our own baby boy came skipping into our lives. His arrival quickly wiped the self-righteous smile off my face as I got to grips with this new rough and tumble world. Before long I was running back to the very friends I had so smugly dismissed just a few years before to seek their advice.

Theory vs practice

One of the problems that any new parent faces is that they are constantly invited to measure their success (or lack of it) against the manufactured images of family life that dominate the media. Endless television shows, the Internet, cinema, billboard ads and magazines portray dads who are strong but caring, high-earning but always available – it's pretty easy to get conned into thinking you're not doing it right.

Lesley Anne Page, a UK professor of midwifery, describes three mythological beings – the perfect father, mother and baby – that many new parents are convinced can (and do) exist. In the cold light of day we know it's ridiculous to think that real people are ever like this, but it's all too easy to be sucked in to an idealized and ultimately sterile view of family life. We can feel twinges of disappointment and self criticism when our own version doesn't seem to come up to scratch.

The truth is that a typical family day is often much more like an episode of *The Simpsons* than we'd ever care to admit. Remember – even the beautiful couple with the designer-clad baby, who live down the road and seem to have it all sorted out, still have their fair share of anxieties, failures and disappointments. No one is immune. But from the outside we only ever get to see a small part of a much bigger picture.

A bit of perspective

The sooner you come to terms with the myth of the perfect parent, the freer you will feel to develop into the father that you know you can be. Remain realistic and don't try to attain the unachievable. After all, none of our kids came with a personalized user's manual.

Even veteran dads with grown-up children admit that they're still making it up as they go along. Remember that as a parent you are on a stage with no script and no prior rehearsals – not even the most critical audience would expect a perfectly delivered performance. Acknowledging our L-plates can be incredibly liberating. It means we're less intimidated by other dads and the way that they do things; we're more prepared to ask for advice and opinions from other, more experienced fathers; and we're less prone to beat ourselves up over minor failures or setbacks. Accepting that the perfect dad doesn't exist in real life can be a huge weight off your mind.

> Parenting books. Check. Antenatal sessions booked. Check. Healthy food. Check. Energy drink. Check. Having a clue. Er... #Lplatedad

Just because attaining perfection as a dad is beyond all of us, there's no reason why you can't be a fantastic, successful father – one that your child is proud of. It takes time, hard work and a lot of patient persistence, together with a willingness to ride out the bumps and accept a few mistakes and disappointments. It's a lifelong learning process.

Myth buster

Despite what some firms would have you believe, this 'perfect family' doesn't exist:

- **Perfect Father** adjusted to parenthood and became the perfect dad over night. He gazes lovingly at Perfect Baby and Perfect Mother all of the time when he's not working at his perfect, stress-free job. He is enormously helpful to Supermum (not that she needs it). He never, ever loses his temper or shouts and is always immaculately turned out.
- **Perfect Mother** looks like she stepped out of a cosmetics advert. She had a Perfect Birth and bonded with Perfect Baby in seconds. Within hours she was back to her pre-birth weight and perfect figure. Her hair, make-up and clothes are always beautiful and her house is spotless. She never feels exhausted or miserable, or wishes that she hadn't had the baby. She never stays in her pyjamas until lunchtime. Or teatime.
- **Perfect Baby** gains exactly the right amount of weight every week, rarely cries, slept through the night from week one and smiles constantly. He is always endearing, sweet, cooperative, quiet and loveable and does not require his parents to make any changes to their well-organized lives.

Condensed idea
Don't beat yourself up striving for perfection – there's no such thing as the perfect dad

(4) A flying start

During the fun part, one of your sperm stepped up
to the mark and made a remarkable effort to fulfil its
purpose. During the following few weeks, the fertilized
egg will develop quickly into a foetus; by week 12 of
the pregnancy he'll have all of his parts and organs.

Half and half

While conception might not normally be on your top 10 list of things to
think about, this is a good time to brush up on some of the biology you
learned in school. During a woman's period, her uterine lining thickens
and ripens, a tiny egg is prepared and friendly cervical secretions smooth
the path in the hope that an intrepid sperm will come whizzing along
and run smack into it.

While you're having a last hug with your partner before falling asleep
(or falling out of the office stationery cupboard, if you're that kind of
guy), that single, lucky sperm penetrates through the outer layers of your
partner's egg and a microscopic, new bundle of cells starts to work its
way down the fallopian tubes. The 23 chromosomes (genetically coded
material) from your partner have joined with the 23 chromosomes you
kindly provided, to create a brand new entity that has 46 chromosomes.
These will pass on all sorts of hereditary traits, some good and some
not so good. The gender of your future baby is also determined in this
'crash' moment, based on whether the victorious sperm contained a Y
sex chromosome (boy) or an X sex chromosome (girl). The chromosomes
are made up of DNA (Deoxyribonucleic Acid, in case you're interested or
want to impress others with your scientific knowledge). All of the DNA in
a cell make up the genome.

The thin blue line

In the first 24 hours after fertilization, the newly formed two-celled organism takes some time out to relax. It will repeat this pattern – work, relax, work, relax – in an uncanny imitation of its male progenitor right through the pregnancy. It grows like crazy then takes a long rest (the cellular/cytological equivalent of going for a drink to mull things over), allowing all the changes to integrate. After its first short break, the fertilized egg goes through an amazing growth spurt, dividing into 64 cells by day three and nearly 500 cells by day five.

Implantation into the uterus occurs around day eight. At this point the fertilized egg begins to secrete the pregnancy hormone hCG (Human Chorionic Gonadotropin – another impressive name to keep in your back pocket), which is the hormone that makes the pregnancy test develop a blue line and send everyone into a bit of a spin.

Chromosome fun facts

Chromosomes are clever bundles of DNA and protein that pass on a bunch of hereditary traits from you and your partner to your baby. These genetic footprints are also super cool in other ways:

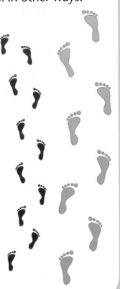

- If you unfolded the DNA in a cell's nucleus, it would be 2 m (6½ ft) long.
- Humans are thought to have around 100 trillion cells (which is a figure that's even higher than the bank bailouts of 2008. Just.)
- If you could stick together all the DNA from all the cells in one person's body, it would string out to about 200 billion km (125 billion miles).
- Humans have only two sets of chromosomes, but wheat has four and strawberries have a whopping 10!

Counting the weeks

The way doctors and midwives count pregnancy weeks seems quite alien to the rest of us, because 'week one' happens before anyone knows anything about being pregnant. Basically, the counting starts from your partner's last menstrual period, not from the moment of conception. So by the time she's one week late for her period, she's already considered to be four weeks pregnant. Luckily you won't have to worry about this too much, because in all likelihood your partner will soon get to grips with the week count and you'll be able to follow her reliable lead.

A new heartbeat

During the next few weeks, the fertilized egg really gets going. The first thing it does is to develop into two distinct parts: one part will go on to become the embryo (and eventually the baby), while the other begins to form the placenta, a large, magnificent filter that sits between the mother and the baby, making sure all the good stuff in her blood gets through, while keeping out the bad. In goes all the important nutrients, hormones, electrolytes and antibodies that the baby needs, and out comes everything that the baby doesn't want (its waste products), all via this incredible blood filtering system. The placenta also protects the baby from the mother's immune system – allowing her body to recognize the growing embryo as a kind of foreign graft without rejecting it.

> This baby – it's definitely happening. Time to man up and take responsibility – ready to teach him about life (skateboard already ordered). #activedad

By the start of the fifth week, the fertilized egg is about the size of a poppy seed. By the sixth week, a primitive heart begins to beat, and a small, rudimentary circulatory system begins to form, along with a backbone. By week eight a small face and tiny rudimentary fingers and toes are visible. By the end of the first trimester (12 weeks) the foetus is the size of an apricot, and all the body parts and major organs have formed. The muscles respond to brain signals, and the foetus is beginning to stretch and move on his own. Your baby is now all systems go!

Condensed idea
Your baby grows from zero to practically fully formed in 12 weeks

5 Her first few weeks

Whether planned or unplanned, this pregnancy will give you and your partner a lot of things to consider and talk about. By engaging with what's going on for her and her changing body you can begin to participate in this new life from its earliest stages.

Trimesters

A normal pregnancy lasts around 37 to 42 weeks, or an average of 40 weeks from the first day of a woman's last period. Statistically babies rarely come exactly 'on time' in the 40th week, but a pregnancy is split into three time stages known as 'trimesters'. These are a useful way of describing and understanding the changes that take place. The first trimester is 1–12 weeks, the second 13–27 and the third 28–41 weeks.

Sick and tired

Not everyone discovers they are pregnant at the same time within the first trimester. For women who have a regular menstrual cycle, the earliest sign is a missed period. However, some women who are pregnant may still have a very light period. Equally, she may find out later on by using a test or by picking up the signs of early pregnancy. Classically, these include tiredness, feeling sick, peeing more often or having unusually tender breasts. But every woman and every pregnancy is different so some signs may be more prevalent than others.

Many women feel sick, and some actually are sick in early pregnancy – doctors estimate that between 50 and 90 per cent of all pregnant women will experience 'morning sickness'. And despite its name, it can actually

Your first 12 weeks

- Although you may not be ready to tell the world yet, choose one or two good friends whom you trust and know really well (perhaps your own dad) to talk to about this new life-changing news.
- Do your bit to help your partner reduce her morning sickness symptoms: plenty of rest, eating little and often and avoiding smells that make her nauseous.
- If your partner is struggling to keep any food or fluid down, encourage her to see her GP or midwife.
- It's best for a mum not to drink alcohol during pregnancy. You could consider adjusting your own alcohol intake to help her reduce hers.
- Smoking is bad news for babies. Support your partner by both trying to give up together.
- Begin to think – and talk with your partner – about attending scans and the birth itself. Be honest about your anxieties but be prepared to face up to them.

happen at any time throughout the day or night. In particular, certain smells and tastes may make her nauseous so try to be sensitive to what they might be. (The favourite late night kebab or curry, for example, might be a 'no no' for a while, unless you want a lot of clearing up to do.) Some foods that seem totally inoffensive to you (meat, chicken, eggs) might suddenly make her queasy. If the sickness is very frequent, she might start feeling quite despairing about the pregnancy, so be ready to reassure her that most women are free of morning sickness once they get past the first trimester, and find ways to help her hang on in there.

It might be helpful to point out that research shows that women who suffer severe morning sickness are less likely to have low-birthweight babies or miscarry – so that's definitely good news. Eating small snacks throughout the day can help, so buy a few bags of unsalted rice cakes or pretzels for her to keep in her handbag or by the bed (she'll probably want to eat something on waking – this often stops the nausea). Ginger tea sometimes works like magic. This is because when ginger is heated or cooked, one of its constituents transforms into a molecule known as zingerone, which binds to neural receptors in the brain and confuses it. It's impossible for someone to 'think about' nausea and ginger at the same time, so put ginger biscuits and tea on your shopping list.

> Shopping list reads: 'folic acid, fruit, high-fibre cereal and listening ear'.
> #emotionalintelligence

Emotional ups and downs

As the first trimester continues, you might notice that your partner's emotional highs and lows become magnified. The slightest thing can make her weep (this even includes TV commercials) or fall about laughing. Don't worry – she's not going crazy, she's just pregnant. Hormonal changes are affecting her neurotransmitters (chemical messengers in the brain), which – coupled with the scariness of being pregnant, which she'll feel no matter how much she wanted this – add up to an interesting combination, to say the least.

Your partner may want to spend a lot of time sleeping, and not with you. Don't assume this means anything other than she's tired – making a baby from scratch is an exhausting business, and it's literally taking a lot out of her. Think about taking the initiative and giving her a bit more space than normal, while being on hand to help out when she feels at her most shattered. Be there, but don't be intrusive (think like a butler). Sensitivity now will definitely earn you a brownie point or two.

Adapting lifestyles

This will also be the time when your partner will be getting to grips with adapting her lifestyle to give your baby the best start. Stopping smoking and cutting down on her alcohol intake (ideally cutting it out) are two of the big ones and she will welcome your support if she needs to do so. A healthy, high fibre diet, including folic acid supplements, will also be an important part of keeping your partner fit and healthy.

Help her keep active, too. Walking, swimming and cycling are perfect ways to exercise and you can do these together. Or apart – if that's what she wants! Suggest but don't push, and be ready with big hugs at all times.

Condensed idea
This can be a tough time for your partner, so try to be understanding of her needs

6 Sex in pregnancy

When it comes to sex, a man's response to his pregnant partner can differ from one guy to the next. It's not uncommon for an expectant dad to go off sex during pregnancy. Alternatively you may find your partner's ever-changing body a complete turn-on.

Can you do it? (Yes you can)

First, let's get the facts straight. It's perfectly safe to have sex during pregnancy, both for your partner and the unborn child. If you're having a normal pregnancy there's no reason why you can't continue to enjoy the regular sex life you had pre-conception, if that's what you both want to do. The exception to this may be if your partner has a history of cervical weakness, a low-lying placenta, bleeding or some other complicating factor, in which case it's a good idea to check with your doctor or midwife first.

> Debbie's suggested getting more creative in our love life. Must check the strength of the chandelier in the living room. #Ishouldbesolucky

Whether you want to have sex, however, can be a different matter. Some couples find it very enjoyable during pregnancy, while others simply feel that they don't want to as often (or perhaps at all), or limit it to the early or middle stages when it might be physically easier. Pre-pregnancy, sex is likely to have been an important part of your relationship so when it changes in terms of when, how and how often, be prepared for it to affect you both in different ways and to differing degrees.

It's very common for dads to experience a dip in their levels of desire throughout their partner's pregnancy. This can often be attributed to four common factors: worrying that it could damage the baby in some way (it can't); concerns for their partner and their baby's health; feelings of apprehension about becoming a dad themselves; or that it simply 'feels wrong' to make love in the presence of their unborn child.

Women, too, find that their sex drive fluctuates tremendously throughout pregnancy. It's common for women to want sex less during the first trimester as this usually coincides with nausea, tiredness, tender breasts and frequent trips to the toilet, none of which appear in the book of 'World's Top 10 Sexiest Things'. On the other hand, research shows that the second trimester is a time when women feel the most sexual desire, only for it to take a dip again in the third as the prospect of birth and labour – and the practicalities of a large belly – begin to take hold.

For some couples, pregnancy has the effect of lighting the touch paper as far as sex is concerned. Many men love the changing nature of their partner's body – beautiful complexion, fuller breasts and rounder hips – and neither of you has to worry about contraception as it's way too late for that. Women are of course free from their periods and, due to the increased blood flow to the pelvic region, often discover that they can be more easily sexually aroused.

How, when and where?

If you have a normal pregnancy, and if you both want to, you can keep having sex right up until your partner's waters break. But this is a time to be especially sensitive to your partner's needs and desires, and to let her guide you.

- Don't let sex become an issue – make sure you talk about it, but pick the right time and the right place.
- She's in the best position (literally) to judge what feels good or not, so follow her lead.
- Don't be afraid to get creative – explore other ways of pleasing each other without penetration.
- Never underestimate the power of a romantic gesture. Hold hands whenever you can if it feels natural; pay your partner compliments and remember that small acts of kindness will show that you love and support her.

Let's talk about sex

It's not unusual to find it difficult to talk openly about sex, especially if you've rarely spoken about it with your partner before. But during these changing, emotional and responsibility-filled times, clear and honest communication is as important as ever. It provides each of you with a positive outlet for your feelings and the opportunity to tackle problems together before they threaten to overwhelm you. There's no need to hop onto the virtual psychiatrist's couch every time you open your mouth, but it's OK to be honest about your sex life – rampant or dormant – and how it's affecting you.

Many couples don't say anything for fear of hurting their partner's feelings, but if you can pick the right moment to talk about things that are going on in your sex life, then you won't have to bury issues that might be worrying you. Resist the temptation to keep your anxieties to yourself – when a problem goes underground it's all too easy for distance to arise in your day-to-day relationship with your partner.

Get creative

While sex is safe for most couples in pregnancy, it may not always be easy. As the pregnancy advances you will need to be more imaginative about positions for lovemaking. This can be a time to explore and experiment together, finding new and different ways to make love.

Your partner may find sex with you on top uncomfortable quite early on, not just because of the bump but because her breasts might be tender. It may be better to lie on your sides, facing each other or with you behind her. If you don't want penetrative sex, try caressing each other to climax, or give each other a sensual massage. Use baby oil rather than aromatherapy oil, as some are unsuitable at certain stages of pregnancy.

Finally, don't forget that cuddles and kisses on the sofa can be just as loving and intimate as 'full' lovemaking, so make the most of these until you're both ready to resume your normal sex life. You never know, you might end up in the mood for full sex – or oral sex if you prefer – after all.

The best advice is to be creative and to keep communication levels to a maximum throughout. The more you work together on this, the better chance you'll have of finding a solution that works for both of you.

Condensed idea
Sex in pregnancy can be great if you keep communication open and honest

7 You and your dad

Parenthood stirs up thoughts about our relationship with our own fathers. The connections we have with our dads run deep and help to shape the people that we are. With fatherhood beckoning, you have an opportunity to develop into exactly the dad you want to be.

A chip off the old block

Your relationship with your own dad may be good, or it may not. He may still be alive, or have died many years ago. You may not even know who your dad is. But whatever the truth of these things for you, your dad's influence, either by his presence in or absence from your life, will have been profound and deep. It will have helped to shape you into the type of person that you are today, and at no time will you be more aware of this than when you face parenthood for the first time.

> My father had a profound influence on me, he was a lunatic.
> #thegreatSpikeMilligan

When you become a dad it's natural to reflect on your own experiences as a child and to expect, for good or bad, that you are likely to follow in (at least some of) your father's footsteps. After all, as you've got older you may have noticed yourself developing mannerisms, attitudes, even physical attributes that are very much like your dad. From time to time, people may have commented that 'you're just like your father' – whether it's your facial expressions or your sense of humour. The mixture of genetic inheritance and learned behaviour can result in surprising similarities.

At the same time, however, your father needn't be your only or even primary role model for your own style of parenting. He's just one influence on what kind of dad you want to be, and will become. There are likely to have been other men who have played positive and significant parts in your (and perhaps your partner's) childhood, adolescence and even adulthood – grandfathers, brothers, uncles, friends, coaches, teachers, youth leaders and so on.

Each of these people provides a well of experience for you that, with some thought and positive reflection, you can draw upon. Think about the traits and characteristics you admired in the men you knew when you were growing up, and follow the example that they have set you.

Becoming dad

If you had a relationship with your father when you were a kid, reflect on what he did for you.

- Write down the things that your father did and you would like to copy. What did he do well, as a dad?
- Write down the things that you would like to avoid.
- Convert the second list into positive actions – things that you will do in order to make things better than they were for you!

Learning lessons

Ask yourself what your dad taught you and what you learned from him. How, for example, did he deal with difficult situations? How did he treat other people? As you think about him in this way, you may realize that he served his family the best way he knew how. So perhaps he wasn't perfect – but maybe he owned his mistakes in a way that inspired you to want to be like him. On the other hand, you might come to the conclusion that your dad didn't do such a great job – his best shot at fatherhood may not have been everything that you wanted it to be. Be aware of those shortcomings and think about how you can do better. Before you know it you'll have the beginning of a dad's job description with your name at the top of it.

One generation on

Have you ever considered that, once upon a time, your dad was in the same boat as you are now? Different circumstances maybe, but he too thought about his new responsibility and had hopes, fears and desires as he waited expectantly... for you!

If your dad's no longer around, talk to other people about him, particularly anyone who knew him when you were a baby. Try to discover what he was really like at that time, slowly unpeeling the layers beneath the image – mentally putting yourself into his shoes for a while. What do others think he would want to say to you now? If you are in touch, ask your dad what it was like for him. Ask him about the circumstances of your birth – how he found out your mum was expecting you, his reaction to that news, how he coped with the early days, and so on. Ask him what his advice now, with hindsight, might be to his younger self.

In either of the above scenarios, it might take a little bit of time and effort to loosen up the brain cells. If you talk to your dad directly, the very fact that you are asking his opinion (without also asking for money) may well take him by surprise, but nine times out of ten you'll find that pressing on will reveal

> Just watched a game with dad and wondered for the first time whether he actually likes footie. #dadseh?

new sides and wisdom to your dad that you've never fully appreciated before. You never know what you might find out and it could be a rewarding experience for both of you.

Over the coming months and years you'll be making many family choices, important and trivial, just like he once did. So draw on the best of all your experiences, learn from your father and leave the negative stuff behind. As you do so, you'll be creating your own identity as a dad, possibly one that would never have occurred to your father, but one that you can certainly be proud of.

Condensed idea
With some work you can be any kind of dad you want to be

8 You and your partner

The arrival of a baby inevitably changes the dynamics in the relationship with your partner, with wonderful but profound shifts in your priorities. You'll need to prepare together and look after each other carefully as you get ready for the uncertainties ahead.

You, me and baby makes three

The amazing introduction of a new life will have a profound impact on the way that your relationship with your partner works. You are moving from two individuals who have fun together to a family of three, with all sorts of new responsibilities. Like it or not, things will never be the same again. Ultimately, it's going to be great, but initially it can take some getting used to.

Couples respond to their new roles in different ways. Some are beside themselves with excitement and unable to wait for the big day to arrive. Others find it more of a reflective or anxious time, wondering about how they'll cope with being responsible for someone else's life and wellbeing. Some women say that they are afraid of losing a sense of who they are, and you may find your partner feels this too. Although she will be getting lots of attention – from doctors, friends and family being excited for her and so on – it can be easy for her to feel that it's the baby who's the real focus of attention, not her.

You too may have times when you feel hurt, jealous or left out if you start to feel that all your partner thinks about is the baby, or if she has strong support from other women such as mothers, sisters and friends, while your own support, especially at this stage, is less obvious.

Under pressure

These can be exciting days for your relationship but challenging ones too. Understanding and patience will get you through the bad times.

- Be honest with each other.
- Encourage each other that you're doing a good job.
- 'Waste' time with each other.
- Ask your friends for advice, but not too many or too often.
- Take responsibility when you need to for issues that arise.
- Ask for forgiveness and be ready to forgive.
- Focus on ways to make things better, not on what went wrong.
- Know when to be quiet with each other.
- Tell your partner you love her, sometimes using words.
- Keep your outside interests alive.
- Keep working at it – never stop communicating.
- Have fun!

All of these feelings are perfectly normal – everyone feels them to a greater or lesser degree – and it may help to talk to others who have been through it. As ever, communicating – and, when necessary, forgiving – each other is the key to keeping things in perspective and to finding ways of making it work.

Look after each other

During this time, when tiredness, responsibility and hormones are all kicking in, keep a special eye out for hotspots and flare-ups in your relationship and resolve to deal with them.

If you know that you need a few minutes downtime when you first get in from work, talk about it. If you know that it is a source of huge irritation to her that you leave the cap off the tube of toothpaste, make an effort to stop doing it. The truth is, even if you don't live together, your baby will have her best start in life if her mum and dad work together as a team.

Make time for each other

Like most things in life, relationships flourish when you give time to them. When you're exhausted or stressed it's tempting to assume that as long as you love each other, everything's going to be fine, whereas in reality your communication levels have dipped to little more than 'Can you pass the remote control?'. As you both prepare for mum- and dad-hood first time around, make sure that investing time in each other is one of the highest things on your to-do list.

Get out and about together. Go for walks, out for a meal, see a film or visit friends. If necessary make a deliberate decision to reduce your involvement in other things – work, sport, your social life – for a little while to spend time together. Stay in too, having 'lie-ins', long breakfasts poring over the papers, and evenings with the TV off. Talk about your hopes, your fears, your dreams, your anything you like.

They say that the difference between a good restaurant and a great restaurant is the little touches. In your relationship, too, it's the little touches that, at the right time, can make all the difference. Thoughtful acts and romantic gestures – from holding hands and spontaneous

DM @Rose. Thought you looked fantastic today. Really beautiful. Can't wait to see you later. xxx

kisses, to a loving text; from running a bath or offering a foot massage; from a tidy house to a timely meal; from an evening out to an evening in. You get the picture – whatever works for you.

When you do get time to yourselves, make a deliberate effort not to always talk about the baby. Your lives, for a time at least, will revolve around your son or daughter soon enough so make sure that not every conversation is about them, leaving yourself room to concentrate on other things and on each other.

Work as a team

Whatever you do, try to view Project Baby (version 1.0) as a team enterprise. You'll soon find that your relationship with your partner will be stronger and easier if you are raising this child as a partnership rather than her being the parent and you being a support worker. The truth is parenting as a team can create a deeper bond between couples than you may ever have thought was possible.

Condensed idea
Find time for you and your partner to keep your relationship happy and healthy

9 New and old friends

During your partner's pregnancy, it's important that you work hard at keeping your own social support structures healthy. Your male friendships, particularly with new dads at similar or later stages to you, are particularly vital at this time.

Good dads need good friends

The picture of paternity in the 21st century is as varied as it has ever been: good dads, less-than-good dads, present dads, absent dads, physically-present-but-emotionally-absent dads, social dads, quiet dads, boisterous dads, pensive dads, demonstrative dads, distant dads, practical dads, active dads, passive dads, shouty dads, jokey dads. You will soon be able to add your own adjectives to the list above (my

youngest son has just wandered in and helpfully suggested 'annoying dads').

Along with our differences, however, we have some major similarities too.

> There's a myth that when men get together we can only talk about two things – football and sex. Nonsense. It's football, sex, MONEY and KIDS. #tellingitlikeitis

In his famous book *Men Are from Mars, Women Are from Venus*, John Gray suggested that a key difference between men and women is that, whereas women like to talk openly about their innermost thoughts, feelings and anxieties, men don't. Gray suggests that, on the whole, we prefer to go into a metaphorical 'cave' and work out things for ourselves in peace and quiet. This may be because we're mistakenly trying to be 'strong' (see page 7) with our partners, and perhaps want to look cool to our friends. But this is a time to put pride on one side, get honest and start to be open to some possibly mind-blowing new learning.

Rite of passage

In most cultures, the news of impending fatherhood can generally be regarded as a special 'male moment'. For a split second one man will look at another and sense a connection – a shared understanding that fatherhood represents embarking on a rite of passage to truly becoming 'A Man'. You may find that this is one of the few times when your closest friend turns to you and says 'How are you doing?' and really wants to know.

This is a time that you will really need an invigorating bunch of friends around you. You'll need them to help you complete your own initiation into fatherhood. And you'll also need them to provide a community of men for your sons and daughters to get to know and respect as they grow up – they will help fill in the gaps that you can't fill yourself. You need friends to keep your feet on the ground, tell you to loosen up every now and then, and to puncture your ego whenever they can.

Dads in antenatal

Elsewhere in this book you'll read about how useful antenatal classes or joining an antenatal group can be. They're a great way of understanding with your partner what pregnancy, labour, birth and early parenthood is all about, to ask questions and learn from other people. All the same, they are not always a place where a guy feels naturally at home or at his most comfortable.

Some antenatal teachers are brilliant at making every session as inclusive as possible for the dad and the mum, but the fact is, the dynamic of a mixed environment talking about parenthood is bound to be entirely different to an all-male (or all-female) group. So early on, try floating the idea of a 'boys only' evening as part of your programme – all the men may be thinking it, but it might take you to suggest it.

Building a network

Having good friends around you will help you stay sane and be a better dad, so make time for them – both old friends and new.

- Find one or two people you can really talk to, as well as ones you can have a laugh with.
- Consult friends across the generations – the wise voice of experience is priceless.
- Book time for seeing friends into your diary and don't cancel for work reasons.
- Be careful not to isolate your partner, but help her to see that you need space too.
- If you join an antenatal class with your partner, arrange with the other dads to meet up occasionally.

Online communities

There is an ever-increasing array of fantastic websites and online social networking tools for dads. These provide a ready source of useful advice and allow you to ask your burning questions with the cloak of anonymity that the Internet provides. If that's your thing, go for it, but be careful not to rely on this as your only source of support. Nothing can ever beat sitting down with someone who knows you well and talking to them, really talking about the things that excite you (and worry you) about becoming a dad.

> These days I love it when the inlaws visit. They get to look after the little one while I go out! #cheekybuttrue

Keep the friendships going

When the baby arrives, it is going to have the impact of a train crash on some areas of your life – and is especially likely to squeeze 'time with mates' off the schedule. It might seem as though suddenly there aren't enough hours in the day to work and look after your baby and partner, let alone get together with friends. At the same time your single mates – who are just as important to your sanity and wellbeing as your 'new-dad friends' – might assume that you're too preoccupied to go out with them any more. So consider telling your friends now that over the next year or so you may disappear into the world of parenting for several weeks at a time, but if it's too long, to come and get you. If you're going to be a great dad, you need to remember to have fun outside the home too.

Condensed idea
Make the most of old friends and new as you journey into fatherhood

10 Growing baby

The second trimester (13–27 weeks) is a huge period of growth for your baby and a time when your partner's body is adapting significantly to the rapidly developing little person within it. This is the time for you to get fully involved with this pregnancy and new life.

13–16 weeks

By the time your partner reaches the second trimester, the speed of growth of your unborn baby is really gathering pace. By week 13 or 14, nourished by the placenta, your baby will be almost 7 cm (3 in) long from her head to her bottom and will even have her own fingerprints.

By 16 weeks she will be beginning to look like a tiny baby, and her digestive system, liver, kidneys and lungs will be beginning to mature. She will be becoming sensitive to light and her ears will have developed, although she won't be able to hear yet. Her shoulders, back and temples will be covered in soft, fine hair called 'lanugo' which protects her and usually disappears sometime before birth.

From about 16 weeks it will be possible to tell the sex of your baby, and towards the end of this stage the midwife will be able to hear her heartbeat using a small listening device placed on your partner's stomach.

17–20 weeks

This is a busy time for your baby's growth. By week 18 she will have doubled her weight since the start of this trimester, now weighing in at an impressive 140 g (5 oz) or so, and measuring around 13 cm (5 in) from

the top of her head to her bottom. The placenta will be getting bigger
to keep pace with the baby's requirements. It is also about this time
that your baby's body will begin to be covered with 'vernix', a greasy
substance that coats and protects her skin, forming a waterproof layer.

By week 20 your baby's body will have grown bigger and it is now more
in proportion with her head. Hair, eyelashes, eyebrows – even taste buds
– are all forming and she will be able to yawn, stretch and make facial
expressions. Her reflexes have also developed. Your partner may begin
to feel the baby moving but don't worry if she doesn't feel anything yet.

21–23 weeks

Now she'll feel something! Your baby will enter her most active stage
yet from around 20 weeks – twisting, turning and kicking. Get used to
the occasional 'oof!' and 'ow!' as your partner is subjected to an internal
gymnastics display – if you're lucky you'll be able to feel it for yourself.

By week 21 most babies can hear sounds, so it's a great time to start
talking and even singing to her. In the coming weeks she will get to
know – and be soothed by – the sound of her mum's and dad's voices.

What's in a name?

The second trimester is a good time to begin to think about what to call your baby. A name is a powerful part of a person's sense of him or her self, so take the time to think about this at length. There are lots of baby name books on the market to help you play around with ideas, and plenty of ideas on the web. Start by asking yourselves the following kinds of questions:

- Do you want to name the baby after a friend or family member?
- Do you have any names that are personal favourites?
- Would you prefer a name that has a meaning?
- Would you prefer a religious name, or something that is culturally significant?
- Do you want a conventional spelling or something unique?
- Do you want a name that is easily shortened or that has a nickname associated with it? Be careful of initials and the things they can spell.
- Does the name you prefer go well with your second name? (I'm thinking of those old favourites, like Joe King, Aretha Holly and Evan Keel.)

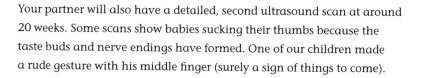

Your partner will also have a detailed, second ultrasound scan at around 20 weeks. Some scans show babies sucking their thumbs because the taste buds and nerve endings have formed. One of our children made a rude gesture with his middle finger (surely a sign of things to come).

At 22 weeks the baby will be about 500 g (1 lb) in weight and may show signs of responding to certain sounds. By the 23rd week her hearing will be well established and she will be able to make out certain noises such as your partner's heartbeat, and she will be able to recognize and respond to you and your partner's voices. By now, her hands will be able to grasp – some babies occasionally grip the umbilical cord.

24–28 weeks

From week 24 your baby is considered by doctors to be 'viable'. This means that if she were to be born at this stage she would have a chance of survival, although obviously babies born so prematurely have huge challenges to overcome. By this time she'll be about 20 cm (8 in) long and weigh 600 g (1¼ lb) or so.

Over the next four weeks your baby will rapidly gain weight. By week 25 or 26 her eyelids will open and at this stage almost every baby has blue eyes. They will stay this way until a few weeks after the birth when they may change to a different colour. By 28 weeks your baby's chances of survival outside the womb have moved up from 60 per cent (at week 25) to 90 per cent. She will have grown

> Who'd have thought it – there really IS a baby in there!
> #learningasIgoalong

to about 35 cm (14 in) in length and may be beginning to open her eyes. And in the dark of the womb, when she doesn't seem to be kicking around so much, she may well be dreaming; this is thought to start around week 27.

By now your daughter will have periods when she sleeps and periods when she's wide awake – and your partner will know exactly when these are, but of course they probably won't coincide with when she wants a rest.

Condensed idea
Familiarize yourself with the weekly development timetable of your baby

(11) She's back!

The second trimester is the time when many women begin to really enjoy their pregnancy as the risk of miscarriage diminishes and morning sickness subsides. This is a period of huge growth for your baby and enormous change for your partner.

The passing of week 12 is a significant hurdle when the chances of miscarriage decrease significantly, and will be greeted with understandable relief by you and your partner. She'll probably feel more energetic, less nauseous (although for some women morning sickness can go on longer) and have less tender breasts at this point, too.

Around now, her bump will just be beginning to show. You may begin to notice the famous 'pregnancy glow' as your partner's hair looks glossier and her skin healthier. This is the part of pregnancy that many women say they enjoy the most – when they're enjoying the sensation and physical benefits of being pregnant, but the baby is not yet so big that it introduces other practical challenges.

Your partner may show extra skin pigmentation too – her nipples will darken and, for many women, a dark line will develop from her navel to her pubic hair. This 'linea nigra' is caused by pregnancy hormones and will fade, along with other spots of darker skin, after the baby is born. It's a good, healthy sign, so tell her not to worry.

Hormonal changes will continue to create some interesting symptoms – a stuffy nose, the occasional nosebleed and bleeding gums are just a few. Nosebleeds in particular are pretty common but encourage your partner to tell her doctor or midwife if she has more than one or two.

Hearing the heartbeat

At 17–20 weeks, your partner will probably become hungrier than usual. Her back may hurt, her tiredness increase and she may even become breathless now and then. At the same time she'll probably seem happier and more confident as her bump becomes more noticeable and she starts to feel the baby move. The hormones

> Properly felt the baby move today. Saw it too – watching @Jenny's stomach moving with a life of its own. #bizarrebutawesome

will continue to be as active as ever and, as a result, your partner will probably become a bit clumsy or forgetful. At night-time, when her movement isn't rocking the baby to sleep, she may feel the occasional reassuring wriggle inside her as he flexes his tiny arms and legs.

This is also the time when your partner might notice the appearance of the dreaded stretch marks. Just about every pregnant woman gets them and so, apart from eating a healthy diet to avoid gaining unnecessary weight, there's little she can do to avoid them. Even the most expensive 'miracle' creams are unlikely to make much of an impact so it may simply be a case of reassuring you partner that, stretch marks or not, you love her just the same.

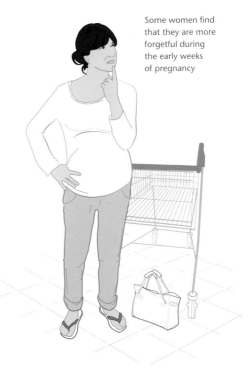

Some women find that they are more forgetful during the early weeks of pregnancy

Decisions, decisions

As you approach the halfway point, it's time to think about the best ways you can support your partner. Here are some ideas.

- Make sure you know how the pregnancy affects your partner at different stages, so you have an idea of what help she might like.
- Do your best to be at the scans – they're a fantastic experience for you and a practical way of showing support for her.
- Take decisions together but if you really can't agree, go with your partner's preferences – after all, it's her body.
- Decide together whether you would like to find out if it's a boy or a girl – remembering it's not 100 per cent accurate.
- Think about where your partner would like to have the baby.
- Make a decision about whether you are going to be at the birth yourself.
- Make sure you talk to your midwife about any worries or concerns.

Emotional MOT

Although your partner will be feeling physically more like her old self (or perhaps, more accurately, her 'new improved self') at this stage, continue to keep an eye on her emotional wellbeing. By week 19 or 20 she will be approaching half way through her pregnancy term – a cause for celebration if ever there was one, but the excitement might well be accompanied by some feelings of trepidation about the stages and choices you have ahead of you. It's completely normal, so make sure you keep talking to one another and to your midwife about anything that is causing concern.

Other people will start to notice that your partner is pregnant and you may encounter the strange experience of complete strangers wanting to touch your partner's emerging bump. Don't be afraid to politely ask them not to do so if it makes you or your partner feel uncomfortable.

From 21–23 weeks, your partner will feel the baby move about more often so her sleep may be increasingly disturbed, making her a bit more absent-minded or forgetful. Not only this, but she will probably have the questionable joys of indigestion, backache, increasing perspiration, swollen ankles (and hands), constipation, a touch of piles, varicose veins and the occasional leg cramp. Probably not the best time to bring up how tough it is being a man sometimes…

Cravings

From weeks 24–28, your partner will probably be feeling more energetic again. Unusual food cravings may kick in. No-one knows what causes them, and there's no harm in satisfying them as long as she doesn't overdo it. Sometimes the craving is for inedible things – soap, earth, chewing on the rubber around swimming goggles – but encourage her to resist the temptation and talk to the midwife instead.

From now on your partner should avoid lying on her back, as the weight of her uterus can restrict the blood circulation. It's also not a great idea for her to stand for very long periods, so encourage her to sit with her feet up whenever she can and be ready to fetch and carry for her more than usual. By the end of week 27 she will be officially into her third trimester. She'll be walking differently because her shape and her centre of gravity will have changed. She's into the home run.

Condensed idea
The second trimester is when your partner will start feeling more 'human' again

Trimester 2 and you

As your partner adjusts to her ever-changing body and you get used to the big day getting closer, there are lots of ways to show support. From joining an antenatal class to eating more healthily, the good news is that by helping your partner you'll be helping yourself too.

Back to school

The second trimester is the time to sign up for antenatal classes. There may be some on offer from your doctor or hospital, or you might choose to join a private group with a particular perspective, such as a 'natural birth' class. Even if you are the keenest expectant father, antenatal classes may not feature highly on your list of things to do on a weekday evening. But if you can set your preconceptions aside you may be pleasantly surprised.

An antenatal group is a great forum for getting your questions answered. It focuses on the practical preparations for labour and parenthood, and classes outline the different types of childbirth, the pain relief that your partner might prefer and what can happen if things don't go to plan. It also gives you a chance to meet other couples who are at the same stage of expectant parenthood as you. As with any group of people facing a life-changing event together, some of the people you meet here may well become friends that you will have for the rest of your lives; friends you'll grow old with while your kids grow up.

> I am the foot massage king!
> #careerchangeperhaps

Eating well

A healthy diet is important during pregnancy, but eating well shouldn't be a chore. You and your partner (join in to make things easier for her) should aim to eat plenty of fruit and vegetables, protein-rich food (such as fish and meat), and high-fibre food (such as pulses). Fibre will help her digestive system cope and keep moving. While she's building a baby she'll need more calcium-rich food too, such as semi-skimmed milk, hard cheese and yogurt.

Some foods should be avoided, including:
- alcohol
- uncooked foods, such as raw fish, meat or eggs
- mould-ripened cheeses
- foods that are undercooked, such as poached eggs
- liver and liver products, such as pâté.

Furthermore, antenatal classes can reassure you – this is especially important if you are nervous about the prospect of the birth. One of the greatest ways that you can help your partner during labour is to be a calm and relaxing presence for her. The more informed you are about the realities of what to expect, the better prepared you will be.

Health Kick

Pregnant women do not need to 'eat for two' – they need no more calories than usual for the first six months and only an extra 200 a day for the final three – but this is not the time to go on a diet either. If your partner already eats a healthy diet, she won't need to make major changes when she's pregnant. There are some nutrients, however, that will be particularly important – folic acid, vitamin D, iron – as well as a few foods to avoid (see box, page 49). One of the best ways that you can support your partner is to adjust your eating habits to mirror her diet. She's going to struggle if she finds you tucking into pie and chips every night while she's eating steamed fish and broccoli. Buying healthy snacks and serving smaller portions will set you both on your way. If you are regular coffee, tea or alcohol drinkers, try to cut down your intake together. Make sure you both drink plenty of water to keep yourselves – and, through your partner, your baby – hydrated.

Keep her moving

Exercise is important when you're pregnant, but your partner may need to make a few changes – moving towards low impact aerobic exercises instead of more intense regimes. Walking and swimming are great throughout the pregnancy, and you're the person best-placed to motivate her to get up and out, if you do it too.

Antenatal classes will tell you exactly how best to support your partner during labour

However, you're also the best person to encourage her to take a rest. A relaxing bedtime routine such as a warm bath or a good book works wonders, and the offer of a foot massage or neck rub will rarely go amiss. Offer practical solutions to help her stay comfortable – keeping your bedroom cool or getting her more pillows to support her bump while in bed. Talking to the baby while she lies down (and he probably wakes up) is a great way for the three of you to connect.

Emotional support

Turn your male emotional intelligence monitor up to 'full'. Your partner may be feeling physically better from midway through her pregnancy but be prepared and sensitive to the fact that the slightest thing may reduce her to tears. Bear in mind that around 10 per cent of women suffer mild to moderate depression during pregnancy. Experts used to think that pregnancy hormones offered some protection against depression, but the current view is that the huge hormonal shift at the start of pregnancy may actually disrupt some brain chemistry and cause depression. If you notice your partner's mood taking a dip, encourage her to talk to you, a friend or her doctor. A woman's emotional health during pregnancy is every bit as important as her physical wellbeing.

Nights out

Soon you'll be parents and it'll be harder to find time for each other, so go out as much as you can before the birth – restaurants, cinemas, whatever you enjoy. Spend time with friends. Put your glad rags on and go out on an old-fashioned date. It's amazing what a few laughs and cuddles can do for your relationship.

Condensed idea
Focus on her needs and desires and you'll both feel better

(13) Who's involved

A small army of highly trained, highly competent professionals will help to manage the safe and successful progress of the pregnancy. This chapter offers an overview of the main people involved and the role that they play in pregnancy, birth and postnatal care.

The midwife

A midwife (which literally means 'together with woman') will be the main provider of care for your partner during her pregnancy, her childbirth and for a short period after her baby is born (usually about 28 days). They are highly-qualified, highly-skilled professionals who qualified first as general nurses, then undertook specialist training as midwives. They ensure that your partner's pregnancy goes as well as possible and that any potential problems are picked up quickly.

Your partner will be probably be introduced to her midwife early on, but depending on your country of residence she may meet a number of different members of a midwifery team throughout her pregnancy. As long as everything remains normal, a midwife can provide all your partner's antenatal care, but if complicating factors arise the midwife may refer her to a specialist doctor, such as an obstetrician or gynaecologist, for further investigation.

Most midwives work in hospitals or in a community health centre, but there are also independent professionals available if you prefer. A hospital-based midwife will work in an obstetric or consultant unit, a birth centre or midwife-led unit. Midwives also staff the antenatal clinic, labour ward and postnatal ward.

Community midwives often work within a team that can help to provide a degree of continuity of care for your partner, but how this works in practice will vary according to where you live. They see women at home and at clinics and might be available for home births. In some cases they will come to the hospital ward when labour begins. Once your baby is born, wherever it happens, a community midwife will visit your partner and your new baby at home for (in the UK) up to 10 days afterwards.

Dads as advocates

As you encounter different professionals during the pregnancy, bear in mind that enabling them to do their job well will help them to better support your partner, your baby and you.

Bedside manner will differ from person to person, of course, but generally the health staff you will meet will be highly professional and caring, expert in their field with years of training and experience behind them.

They will understand if you are worried about your partner or anxious about the baby, but resist the urge to let your anxieties bubble over so that you become, in essence, a stroppy dad. After all, when liaising with hospital staff yours is a vital role – especially in a busy maternity unit – as a calm advocate for your partner and baby. Your role is to speak up for them when they are unable or uneasy about doing so. Chances are you know your partner best, so say what you need to, when you need to – even in hectic scenarios your voice is important. Avoid being overbearing and be ready to step back when necessary and allow the people caring for your partner to use their professional judgment.

A good relationship with your midwife is important, so be prepared to work hard at it. It's vital that both your partner and you have confidence in her skills, and that you know, as best you can (given the realities of pregnancy and birth) that she will support your choices.

From day one, if you possibly can, think of your midwife, your partner and yourself as a team, and encourage your partner to do the same. It's very important that a woman feels safe and relaxed during pregnancy, so knowing that she has the support of a reassuring, responsive and unintrusive midwife (and partner) will make a huge difference.

The doctors

An obstetrician (in Latin it means 'to stand by') is a doctor who specializes in pregnancy and childbirth. In the UK, obstetricians only become involved if there is a problem with your partner's pregnancy or birth (if she needs a caesarean section, for instance). But if everything goes according to plan and is completely straightforward, neither she nor you may ever actually see an obstetrician, unless you're paying for private healthcare.

Another antenatal appointment. Honestly, in this pregnancy I think we've met more doctors than the Daleks! #meetthemedics

A paediatrician is a doctor who specializes in babies and children. A neonatologist is a paediatrician who specializes in newborn babies. If your midwife or doctor has any concerns about your baby's health, they may recommend that a neonatologist is present at the birth.

From time to time, your partner may be asked whether a student (doctor or midwife) can attend one of her appointments as part of their medical training. They are there to watch and learn, but it is perfectly okay to say no if this feels uncomfortable for either of you.

Non-medical specialists

- Doulas (it means 'female servant' in ancient Greek) provide an independent service focusing on giving physical, emotional and practical support to women during pregnancy, childbirth and early parenthood. They are not midwives (they don't do anything medical for example) but they aim to be a continuous and reassuring presence. Many (but not all) doulas have undergone training.
- Healthcare Assistants (HCAs) work within hospital or community settings under the guidance of a qualified healthcare professional.
- Maternity (or sometimes Midwifery) Support Workers (MSWs) assist in the care of mothers and babies, and are under the direct supervision of a qualified midwife.
- Breastfeeding Support Workers do exactly what their title suggests.

Condensed idea
Familiarize yourself with the different roles the professionals play

14 Scans and tests

There are various antenatal tests that are important for determining the health of both your partner and your unborn baby. Tests are split into two general types – screening and diagnostic – and you need to understand what they do and how to interpret their findings.

Types of tests

Screening tests estimate the likelihood that a pregnant woman will give birth to a baby with a certain condition. These tests offer probabilities alone, not definite results, and they are generally used to show which women have a greater chance of having a baby with complications.

Diagnostic tests are used to determine whether or not a baby actually has a particular condition. They may be suggested following a detailed screening ultrasound, which has indicated the need for further investigation. Diagnostic tests carry the possibility of affecting the baby, as they are invasive and carry a small risk of miscarriage.

Screening tests

Screening tests are generally non-invasive – they are usually either scans or blood tests and have no adverse effects on the baby. The most familiar of screening tests is the ultrasound scan, which uses high frequency echoes from sound waves to create an image on a screen. The scan is painless and safe – a gel is smeared on your partner's stomach as she lies on a bed, and a transducer (which looks somewhat like a microphone) is rolled across her abdomen. Occasionally ultrasounds are carried out transvaginally (where a probe is inserted into the vagina).

Most women have two scans, but more will be offered if the pregnancy needs specialist care. The first is carried out at 8–12 weeks and focuses on making sure the baby (or babies!) is inside the womb; establishing an accurate due date; checking the size of the baby and his condition (you will be able to see his heart beating).

> Incredible 2 have 1st picture of junior. What a moment! Scan printout stuck on fridge, computer, facebook, phone. Can't see family nose yet tho. #thatsmyboy

A second scan, known as an anomaly scan, is normally offered at 16–22 weeks. This a detailed ultrasound scan that checks the baby's growth rate, heart rate and the development of various vital organs. It can also tell you the baby's sex, so it's important to talk with your partner beforehand about whether you want to find out or not. However, the information is not always accurate so don't start buying colour-coded baby items based on the scan information alone.

Understanding scans and tests

You should be given written information to read about any test your partner is offered, so you can understand the basic details of what's involved. Before you say 'yes' or 'no' to any test that is suggested, ask questions to make sure you know:

• what the test is for
• whether it is a screening or a diagnostic test
• what it will involve
• how long you will have to wait before getting the results
• in what way you will receive the results (there and then, by letter, in person, or via your doctor)
• what your options might be once you have received the results
• who to talk to after getting the results, should you need to follow them up.

Diagnostic tests

There are a number of diagnostic tests that a pregnant mum may encounter. Among the most common are:
• spina bifida, Down's syndrome, sickle cell and thalassaemia screening
• cystic fibrosis checks
• amniocentesis and chorionic villus sampling (CVS).

Your midwife and doctor will be able to explain all about these. But before you make any decisions about a test, talk with your partner about the implications – what action would you take if a test for a serious condition came back positive? If you and your partner would go ahead with the pregnancy in any case, do you want to subject her and the baby to an invasive test now? Before you make any decisions about a pregnancy diagnostic test, take time to talk with your partner about the implications, making sure you're going in with your 'eyes open'. You may find that you spend time worrying unnecessarily but, in the worst case, you may find you are asked to make a decision about whether or not to continue the pregnancy.

Should I attend scans and tests?

Absolutely! First of all, it's good for your partner and a practical way to show your commitment to her, this pregnancy and your baby. A scan can be a nerve-wracking thing to go through, so it's vital that, if you can possibly make it, you 'man up' and support her. What's more, being present at an ultrasound is a fantastic way to connect with your baby, as you watch him moving round. Many dads say it's the first time they felt a proper bond with their baby. Some hospitals and clinics charge for a printout of the scan so don't forget to bring along some cash just in case.

Maternal health tests

Your partner will be offered a number of tests to check on her and the baby's health. Blood pressure and urine tests will be carried out routinely and she may also be offered a glucose tolerance test to look for gestational diabetes (a type of diabetes that can affect pregnant women). Your partner will also be offered a blood test to screen for infectious diseases, including HIV, syphilis, hepatitis B and rubella immunity (also known as German measles). All tests are optional but are recommended because they help avoid health problems for your partner and the baby.

Condensed idea
Scans and tests are an important part of ensuring your baby's wellbeing

(15) Money stuff

The arrival of a baby, however longed-for, will spark the same reasonable question in anyone's mind: can we afford it? This may not be at the top of your list of things to think about, but getting your financial affairs in order now will be time well spent.

Counting the cost

Babies don't come cheap – according to recent statistics, it currently costs over £200,000 to look after a child in the Western world until they are 21. That's not far off a quarter of a million quid. While you take a moment to pick yourself off the floor as you see the purchase of a Ferrari or two move slightly further away, I should perhaps point out that such figures are based on a variety of factors about childcare, education and lifestyle which may not apply to you. But the point is still well made – it was with only a touch of irony that a friend once suggested to me that he was thinking of naming his child after a particular credit card provider in recognition of the contribution it was going to make to his son's life in the future.

> My wallet's full of pictures, where my money used to be. #brokebuthappy

Plan ahead

In the first year of a baby's life, it's easy for a parent to spend a few hundred pounds on nappies alone, never mind all the other essentials your new child will need. With this in mind, it's easy to see why it is common for parents of a new baby to get into serious debt, so it's wise to get on top of your financial situation before it's put under added strain. Start by discussing these challenges with your partner before you start worrying about them or, even worse, arguing about priorities. If you're both aware of the issues and responsibilities ahead, you'll be more able to tackle them together. Talk through how long you or she plans to take off work, and bear in mind that whoever takes on the bulk of childcare may find it hard to adjust to depending more financially on someone else. These are sensitive issues that transcend the money itself.

Budgeting

Write down your monthly income and set against it a list of your regular monthly outgoings. Then add to your 'spending' list the amount of money you think you spend on other things such as food, petrol, clothes, going out and so on. If the money coming in is roughly equal to the money going out, it will be impossible to factor in the new baby expenses. This means it's time to take a hard look at how you're going

Money tips for new dads

1　Make time to talk about money – your priorities might be very different.
2　Recognize that your spending habits will need to change.
3　Be prepared to disagree about money: don't talk about it when you're angry and don't talk about it all the time, but talk regularly, because things change.
4　See money as a means to an end not an end in itself.
5　Adopt a money sharing system that works for both of you.
6　Don't ignore unmanageable debts.
7　Never borrow more to get out of debt.
8　Set yourself some financial priorities and goals.
9　Plan for the future.
10　Use the experts – but don't leave it too late to ask for help.

to make ends meet. Whether it's the weekly take-away, that rarely used gym membership, or the new TV, something will have to give. Setting a target for how much you want to be able to spend per week or month can often help.

Watch the credit

If you're buying baby equipment, keep an eye on how much you're spending – it's easy for large costs to mount up very quickly before the baby's even arrived. No one wants to be stingy, but use your imagination to think of ways to save money. Be wary of building up large credit card bills that you may have difficulty paying back later. It's also a good idea to pay off as many debts as you can before the baby arrives.

Maternity and paternity pay

If your partner is in employment when she is due to give birth, it's important to know what income you can expect during her maternity leave. Even if she intends returning to work, there is often a shortfall in income while she is on maternity leave and checking this out now will avoid the hassle of doing it later when you both have a baby to look after. By talking to her employer at the right time (and within the legal timescales) about the financial fine print, she could save you both a lot of stress later on. More and more employers are beginning to provide paid paternity leave, but if your employer insists leave will be unpaid, you'll need to take this into account in your financial planning. (Read more on this on page 65.)

Looking to the future

Consider saving for your children from the moment they are born – or even before. If you are in the fortunate position of being able to tuck something extra away, do so, and consider getting professional advice about the best way to do it. Another thing that you may want to consider, probably for the first time, is making a will. You may well be thinking, we're talking about new life here not death! However, making a will ensures that when you die, your child will inherit everything that you want them to, with the minimum of red tape and fuss. There are companies which specialize in preparing wills, or you can buy a will 'off the shelf', so check out your options – it needn't cost very much. Part of the will-making process will involve appointing a guardian(s) for your child, so it's a good time to think about the people you would like to invite to take on this important responsibility.

Condensed idea
Assess your joint finances and priorities and start making plans for the future now

16 Know your rights

With the onset of parenthood and its responsibilities, now is the time to be certain of what your legal rights and responsibilities are as a dad. Making sure you have the latest facts and figures will avoid problems later on and help to take the stress out of early fatherhood.

Rights and responsibilities

Having parental responsibility for a child means that you are legally responsible for your child's life, in very many ways (see box, page 66). In most countries married parents automatically have joint parental responsibility, but this isn't always the case for unmarried mums and dads. Mothers are normally considered to have parental responsibility for their children, but with more and more children being born outside marriage, the landscape is changing.

Investigate your rights and responsibilities if you are not married to your partner or won't be living in the same house or apartment as your baby, because these differ from country to country. You may be able to apply for parental responsibility, which will give you the same rights as a married father, but, at the very least, ensure that your name is included on your child's birth certificate.

Bear in mind that even if you are a non-resident dad with parental responsibility, it won't give you an absolute right to have contact with your child. Also, the mother of your child won't have to consult you on a day-to-day basis about your child's upbringing. However, she will, on the whole, be expected to keep you informed about your child's wellbeing and general progress.

Employment rights

If it applies, make sure your partner has informed her own employer in good time about her pregnancy and that she knows what her financial entitlements will be while she is on maternity leave. Depending on where you live, there will be differing guidelines about when a woman must inform her place of work. They will be readily available, however, so you should be able to access them with minimal effort. Find out about your partner's rights – and responsibilities – as an employee whilst she is off, as well as her rights to return to work, should she so choose, after maternity. Some countries have introduced legislation enabling a woman to ask for flexible working upon her return after childbirth and, even if it does not yet appear in law, more and more employers are recognizing the benefits of providing this flexibility for returning mums.

In the same way, talk to your own employer (if you have one) about your own working arrangements surrounding the birth. If you have any choice in the matter, don't take on new big projects close to when the baby is due. Check out your paternity rights and give your boss plenty

Legal responsibilities

Laws don't normally set out in detail what parental responsibility consists of, but if they did, they might include the following key roles:

- Providing a home for the child.
- Protecting and maintaining the child's wellbeing.
- Disciplining the child.
- Choosing and providing for the child's education.
- Determining the religion of the child.
- Agreeing to the child's medical treatment.
- Naming the child and agreeing to any change of the child's name.
- Accompanying the child outside her country of residence and agreeing to the child's emigration, should the issue arise.
- Being responsible for the child's property.
- Appointing a guardian for the child, if necessary.
- Allowing confidential information about the child to be protected or disclosed.

of notice about what you intend to do. Unfortunately, while most men say that they intend to take time off work after their baby is born, only around 10 per cent of new dads take off more than two weeks. This may reflect the limit of paid paternity leave, and some men also feel that they will be seen as less than serious about their career if they take a month or so off work to adjust to family life. And here lies a dilemma ready to chase most new dads for the next 18 years – how is it possible to be a good dad in terms of being the breadwinner, and also a good dad in terms of the hours you spend with your child? This is the work–life balance conundrum (read more on pages 164–67), and you can expect to be juggling this one for years to come. (On the other hand, practice makes perfect, so by the time you're paying university fees, you'll have be adept at creative solutions.) You might want to find out if you can shift your hours (working from 6 a.m. to 2 p.m. for instance) or days (working four longer days instead of five short ones). If you're genuinely committed to sharing the childcare, think about job-sharing, part-time or freelance work. Some companies are happy to employ

> Looking forward to a fun evening ahead. I love forms. No I really do. #procrastinationexpert

former employees as consultants, giving you control of your working days. Or you could suggest working from home one or two days a week. While it's not possible to look after the baby while working, at least you'll be around, and your voice and occasional cuddles will not go unnoticed.

Live-out dads

If you are not expecting to live with the mother of your child, investigate your responsibilities regarding finances towards the upbringing of your new son or daughter. In the UK, there is a statutory requirement for you to pay towards your child's welfare. Even in countries where this is not the case, many men feel that it is the right thing to do and make a private agreement with the baby's mother. Calculate what you can afford carefully; it's not unusual for fathers to hugely overstretch the amount they offer to pay and then find themselves in financial problems. Be honest and keep communication open. And don't make payments in cash: you may later need to be able to provide proof of payment.

Condensed idea
Knowing your rights and responsibilities will make everything seem more manageable

(17) What's a birth plan?

A birth plan will help you and your partner think through your preferences for the birth and what you definitely don't want. It's also a basis for you to ask your midwife for more information, but be prepared to be flexible, because childbirth is not an exact science.

What to consider

If you haven't written one already, your midwife may suggest that you consider writing a birth plan. This is just a piece of paper on which mums- and dads-to-be write their thoughts about how they would like the forthcoming birth to pan out, based on the mum's medical history, her particular circumstances and, frankly, what's available through the maternity service.

Your partner doesn't have to create a birth plan but, if she does want to, your midwife will be able to help. With important decisions afoot, it's important for all of you to have an input, and for you and your partner to agree on the final plan. Your midwife might give you a special form for your birth plan, or there may simply be space in your medical notes. Some websites

> It's going to be a caesarian after all, but we really don't mind now, we just want that baby safely in our arms. #expectantdad

show other people's birth plans – along with what actually happened at the birth – and these can be useful starting points. The kind of things you need to consider are given in the box on page 70.

Plan A and Plan B

Birth plans are useful because they help expectant parents think through some of the key issues around the birth before they are faced with them in the labour ward or at home. It would be a mistake, however, to consider them as somehow a ticket to the perfect labour. Contrary to popular myth, childbirth is not an exact science – it is a natural process driven by the woman's body and, recent research suggests, by the baby itself.

In addition, midwives and doctors have to make decisions based on the clinical evidence and the resources at their disposal. So although a birth plan is useful for them because it provides a real insight into how, ideally, you'd like things to go, be prepared to adjust your expectations. Labour is an uncharted journey, and you cannot plan for everything that might happen. If things begin to go very differently from the way you want them to during labour, your midwife will try to explain why at the time. If she has had to work quickly, with no time for explanation, she will tell you everything that was involved after she's managed the birth and your baby is safely born.

Birth plan ideas

Talk with your partner about the following kinds of things, and take notes. Things to think about might include:

- Who the birth partner is going to be – this is the person who will accompany mum through her labour (usually the dad).
- Where your partner would like to give birth – home, maternity centre or hospital?
- Your partner's preferred positions for labour and delivery.
- What forms of pain relief she would like to begin with and progress to, if at all.
- How you both feel about assisted deliveries (ventouse or forceps).
- Whether your partner would like a drug such as oxytocin to be used to speed up labour if medical staff suggest this.
- How you both feel about caesarean section (bearing in mind this is only offered when medically necessary) and whether you would want to be present.
- Whether, if necessary, your partner would prefer an episiotomy (surgical cutting of the perineum), or to allow natural tearing should one of these options be suggested.
- Who will cut the umbilical cord?
- Whether your partner wants your baby handed straight to her, or to be cleaned first.
- Which method of feeding your partner would like to try delivering after the birth (breast or bottle).
- Whether you would like a Vitamin K shot for the baby.
- How you both feel about the possible presence of medical students.

Birth partners

Now is the time to decide who is going to be present at the actual birth. For most couples, though not all, this means YOU! The father of the baby. The dads of old who left their labouring wives at the door of the delivery suite and headed off for the pub for a pint and to hand round cigars have almost been consigned to history. The majority of men want to be as involved as possible in the birth itself.

It's likely that everyone will assume that you'll be there at the birth – and you may be happy about that. Equally, however, agreeing to be present at the birth may not, for you, be as straightforward a decision. Many men today often feel under pressure to be at the birth – not necessarily from their partners or the medical staff, but from work colleagues, family and friends. This is a decision that needs some thinking through. It's perfectly natural for a man to be anxious about the labour. If you have strong reservations, or realize that you really do not want to be present, talk to your partner and the midwives who are caring for her. If for any reason you think you won't be there, agree on a birth partner with whom you're both totally comfortable.

If, however, you do decide to go for it (which I hope you will) I guarantee it will be a life-changing experience. I suspect that few dads (and no mums) would say that they truly relished the prospect of attending labour. Many of us took regular breaks for walks round hospital car parks. All of a sudden, though, we found ourselves overwhelmed at witnessing, and participating, in the birth of our children and supporting our partner in this incredible, extraordinary journey.

Condensed idea
Birth plans are useful for discussing what you want, but remember that babies often have other ideas

(18) Already connecting

When it comes to connecting with their unborn child, mums do have the advantage of, let's say, a 'hardwired' link to the baby. Dads on the other hand, have to work a bit harder at building a relationship with their little one and it's never too early to start.

Getting to know you

Many dads don't really feel that they become a father until the day their child is born, but it's possible to start bonding with your child well before that. The huge advantage of this is that you'll feel more at ease with your baby from the day he's born, when you'll greet him like an old friend rather than a stranger. At around 30 weeks into the pregnancy, when the arrival of your first born child is only around 10 weeks away, there's a great chance to really begin to interact with your baby on a new level. Studies have shown that, although he will be able to hear voices from considerably earlier, this is when a baby learns to distinguish between his parents' and strangers' voices.

> Just bought junior his first football shirt. And boots. Size 0–3 months. #waitingforthecallup

Singing your way to his heart

This gives you a golden opportunity to get into a good habit that will serve you well throughout your parenthood journey – hanging out with your kid. It may seem more than a little surreal at first, but overcome the embarrassment of talking – even singing – to your partner's belly and just do it. Each time you say hello to your partner, greet your baby too, and maybe give the bump a gentle pat. You don't need to shout; the very opposite in fact. Keep your voice low and soft, because this will be reassuring and calming for all three of you (amniotic fluid is quite a good conductor of sound).

Over time your baby will become accustomed to your voice and be able to recognize it when he hears it for the first time in the big wide world outside the womb. These 'conversations' will be good for you and your partner too – you can both talk to the baby together. It'll help the baby seem more real and it'll also show your partner that you are committed to being an involved dad from (even before) the start.

Thank you for the music

Recent years have seen growing interest in the possible benefits of playing music to babies in the womb. Many column inches have been expended on whether such early exposure can help to create a homemade musical genius, speed up his language acquisition once he is born or is at least useful for calming him down. Since research on this topic is in its infancy and scientists have yet to reach definitive conclusions, the best advice may be not to worry unduly about this one. If you're going to play music, do so at a reasonable volume and more for your own enjoyment than for any benefits it might confer on the baby. Whether it's Metallica or Mozart, John Lennon or Jon Bon Jovi, play it because you like it and it helps you to perk up, chill out or just have fun. Just remember to change the music occasionally – for everyone's benefit!

Singing might not be your thing, but why not give it a try – even if a whispered version of 'The Ace of Spades' is the only thing that comes to mind? If you decide, however, that the best place for your singing voice really is anywhere but in public, there are lots of other things you can do instead. Read him a story or something from the newspaper; or have a chat, man to man (this will work fine even if 'he' turns out to be a 'she'). Just think, a captive audience – no talking back or asking for money (that'll soon change after he or she pops out, believe me). If you're feeling in a deeper, more reflective mood, try sharing memories from your own childhood and tell the bump about the things you'd love to do with him as he grows up. Tell him how much you love him. After all, there are lots of things to say and your baby has lots of time to listen. But don't get carried away – 15 minutes is plenty, because babies in the womb need plenty of rest.

The name game

Some parents-to-be give their baby a name while in the womb – not their real name but a nickname – as a way of making the baby feel more like a real person rather than just 'the baby'. It can be gender neutral, or if you know the sex, something that fits. Friends of ours called their son 'Diggory' just about all the way through the pregnancy. I haven't a clue why, it just kind of stuck and they still call him that every now and then; it just pops out, even though he's now a strapping 11-year-old called James who is almost as tall as his mum.

Paparazzi your babe

A picture really is worth a thousand words. So get a scan picture if the radiographer offers one and keep it on show – on your fridge or on the bedside table – and look at it often. Carry a photo in your wallet too, or on your phone, and show it to your friends. Men tend to find it hard to get attached to things when we can't see, hear or touch them, and this will help you to feel the reality of your son's life and the reality of your role (which has already started) as his dad.

Feel the Kick

Midway through the second trimester you will be able to feel your baby move or kick – you'll be able to feel how much he has grown as the movements get stronger. Why not listen for his heartbeat too? A reasonable stethoscope or a 'pinard' (a foetal stethoscope shaped a bit like an ear trumpet) can be purchased cheaply online and either of these will provide hours of fun and bonding.

Drop him a line

One dad wrote his daughter an email a day for 10 years, then published them as a book. Not many of us could stretch to that level of commitment, but writing is a fantastic idea. For you, it might be an occasional letter, a diary entry, or a blog even – stored away for a time when your child decides to read them. Write about what happened or what your thoughts were on a particular day, or things that have sprung to mind that you'd like to tell him (before you forget). Imagine if your father had done this for you – what kinds of things would you have found fascinating to read?

Condensed idea
Speaking to your unborn child may feel ridiculous, but it's immensely powerful

19 Worst fears

Fatherhood is a huge step and can feel daunting. It may be tempting to mask any fears that arise because it feels awkward to admit to them, especially at the point where others see you as becoming 'a real man'. However, these anxieties and insecurities are normal.

Is she in love with someone else?

It's not unusual for a new or expectant dad to feel that the baby has already begun to take centre stage in his partner's affections. Grief that he has 'lost' the woman who used to love him sometimes gives way to feeling like a spare part, even to the point of being jealous of the new baby. You'll be relieved to hear that such feelings are completely normal and most dads can expect them to surface from time to time.

After all, there is a new, third person in this relationship that was previously limited to two. So whatever your feelings, get them out in the open. Start by talking

> Turns out hardly anyone dies in childbirth any more. The midwife's taken to calling me Dickens.
> #sorelieved

to your partner as clearly and honestly as possible, but talk to other dads too. Talking to your partner may not always be easy – you may not want to bother her with your problems (after all, she's having the baby) or you may worry she'll see you as too sensitive when she needs a 'strong, supportive male', but talking with her about it will help.

The most dangerous thing you can do is bury your feelings, which over time could damage you and your relationship. In contrast, by spending time talking to each other, you may well discover a new depth to your relationship that brings the two – then the three – of you closer than you ever could have expected.

Will she and the baby be okay?

The feelings of responsibility that well up during labour can at times be overwhelming. We are used to managing the risks we take in life, but we can't manage this one. However skilled and knowledgeable the midwives and medics are (and they are highly skilled and knowledgeable), childbirth is still a nerve-wracking, physical experience. Scary things can happen to the person you love most in the whole world.

However, while childbirth used to be associated with high infant and maternal mortality, that's no longer the case. Regular monitoring of mum and baby – by machines and people – means that problems are noticed and promptly dealt with. Talk to the professionals about your anxieties, because they're the ones who see this every day, and they are there to help you. Ensure that you're well informed too; the more you know, the more likely your fears will lessen. Talk to other dads, particularly those further down the road of fatherhood. Cut to the chase and talk with absolute honesty – I guarantee that they will have had the same anxieties as you.

Has good sex gone forever?

A soon-to-be dad friend of mine cut to the chase recently, asking me whether his wife's breasts would ever return to their former glory and whether they would ever have 'those beach moments again?' (I didn't ask for details). The breasts part is relatively easy. While they will change shape and perhaps be a little less pert than you've been used to, there's every reason that they will be as beautiful as they always were.

As for 'beach moments', it's inevitable that your sex life will change as the pregnancy progresses, but keeping the lines of communication open between you both can make a huge difference. If one of you starts resenting the other – perhaps because she doesn't think you're helping enough, or you feel she's excluding you – and neither of you initiates an honest conversation about it, it's unlikely that you're going to enjoy great sex. This is the time to focus on helping her begin to feel more like her old self again. Work at emotional, rather than physical intimacy. It might seem like a long time to go without sex, but, in truth, you probably won't miss it all that much – you'll be too tired looking after your son or daughter. Take things gently and keep talking about how you both feel – it will give you both a chance to feel like a couple, not just parents. Before you know it, you'll soon be enjoying an even better sex life than ever.

Depression in dads

Keep an eye on yourself. For some men, pregnancy triggers more than just the usual new-dad jitters and they experience symptoms quite similar to postnatal depression. The problem is that traditionally this type of depression is seen as being caused by raging hormones, so men 'can't' be affected. This can lead men to hide their true feelings; they are less likely to seek help for their depression and, consequently, experience their symptoms with growing intensity. If you, your partner or your friends notice that your mood has taken a significant, prolonged dip, or you feel a heightened sense of anxiety, or just feel that you don't seem yourself, take action. Talk to your partner and to your doctor; you owe it to your partner and your baby. Most of all, though, you owe it to yourself. Many dads testify that proper support, education and occasionally treatment helped them to successfully manage their feelings as they adjusted to the prospect of fatherhood.

Babies don't bond couples

Many couples mistakenly think that having a baby will bring them together. But the truth is that a baby can't fix a troubled relationship, at least not in the long term – that's the job of you and your partner.

If you're not feeling stable or good about your relationship, it's important to say so and to work through the issues as soon as possible. The sooner you find a way to work together, the sooner you'll feel more comfortable with the prospect of becoming new parents yourselves. As with every aspect of pregnancy, it's important for you and your partner to speak openly – but honestly and sensitively – about what each of you is feeling, and to agree to work together to find solutions to the challenges that you face.

Condensed idea
Talking to someone about your fears will help dispel them

20 The last three months

During the final trimester, the excitement about the arrival of your first child blends seamlessly with a sense that things really are about to change. The burst of energy that your partner had in the second trimester is ebbing away. It's time to step up the support.

Weeks 28–32

By this time your baby's brain is developing quickly and she'll be becoming sensitive to light; she'll even be able to tell the difference between sunlight and artificial light. She'll be about 38 cm (15 in) in length from head to toe, and weigh about 1.5 kg (2½ lb), but the rate of growth from here on is phenomenal. She won't have much room for the

gymnastics she was doing a few weeks back, but she'll be getting lots of exercise by kicking madly. Her lungs are fully formed and now maturing, and she'll be making breathing movements more regularly.

Your partner is likely to be suffering from indigestion, and may also begin to feel practice contractions known as Braxton Hicks (see box, page 82). She may be experiencing the occasional leg cramp and swollen ankles, so encourage her to drink plenty of water and avoid standing for long periods of time. You may begin to notice that your partner is a little more forgetful and clumsy than usual, so make some practical changes: perhaps nominate an easy, obvious place for you both to dump your keys, wallets and phones when you come home. To add to the discomfort, she'll probably be more tired too, as the growing bump makes sleep difficult. Offer to get her more pillows so that she can sleep on her side with a cushion between her knees, or by her side to support the weight of her bump. Her back will be feeling the strain too, so a gentle massage will probably be gratefully received.

Emotionally, you and your partner may be panicking a little about how much there is still to be done before the baby arrives. She's got enough on her plate right now, so just listen to her and be as supportive as possible. By empathizing with her you might be surprised at how much support and great advice you receive in return.

Weeks 33–36

Your baby will still be gaining weight rapidly and her toenails and fingernails will be growing long. By 36 weeks she'll weigh around 2.7 kg (6 lb) and will still be moving every day (your partner should inform the midwife straightaway if she can't feel anything) but her movements will be restricted because of lack of space. Her head will become 'engaged', which means the widest part of it has passed below her mum's pelvic brim, making the mum's breathing and digestion easier. Unfortunately, pretty much everything else has got harder for your partner. Her belly button probably sticks out now

Braxton Hicks contractions

Named after the doctor who first identified them, Braxton Hicks are often described as 'practice contractions' as your partner's body gets ready for labour. Women often describe them as being a tightening, or a bit like period pains. Bear in mind:

- Not all women experience them, but it's normal if they do.
- They can happen several times a day and normally last for less than a minute.
- No one is yet sure what causes them but there is evidence that they increase the blood flow to the placenta and the transfer of oxygen to the baby.
- They start early in pregnancy but are only generally noticeable later on.
- Dehydration may make them more uncomfortable, so encourage your partner to keep drinking water.
- Braxton Hicks are noticeably different to 'real' contractions in that they are irregular, don't last long, and are fairly weak. They don't get progressively stronger and often stop when your partner moves walks, rests or changes position.

and she'll probably feel puffier (swollen hands, ankle and even face) than ever. Help her to rest with her feet up, and encourage her to drink more (without pestering her). Her higher metabolic rate will mean that she feels hot most of the time – which is great in winter but pretty uncomfortable in summer. Some, but not all, women find that their breasts start to leak a thick, creamy or yellow substance. This 'colostrum' is a baby's first milk, and the leaking is your partner's body preparing to breastfeed.

Your partner will probably have stopped work by now and is likely to be attending antenatal appointments every fortnight or so. She needs lots of rest, because labour is approaching and it's likely to be more punishing than running a marathon.

37–40 weeks

By week 37, your baby will be considered full term, even if she doesn't actually arrive for a few weeks yet. It means that if labour started now, the doctors wouldn't delay it. The fact is babies rarely arrive right on time – most decide to appear between 40 and 42 weeks. While you await the starting gun, though, she'll continue to cook nicely and put on around 14 g (½ oz) every 24 hours. By 40 weeks she'll probably measure

> 5... 4... 3... 2... 1... Here we go. #theadventurebegins

at least 50 cm (20 in) and weigh 3 kg (7 lb) or more. She'll still be covered in white, creamy vernix, but the lanugo (fine hair) will have gone.

Your partner will be feeling very uncomfortable by now, but may also get an urge to start 'nesting'. Out of the blue she may develop a new enthusiasm for preparing the baby's room, or doing washing and cleaning. Enjoy her enthusiasm, but keep an eye on her – make sure she takes plenty of rest too. Her Braxton Hicks contractions may be stronger and more frequent now. Whether you're opting for a hospital birth or not, make sure her hospital bag is packed. Be ready for every eventuality but stay calm – your first child could arrive any day now.

Condensed idea
The third trimester is when the excitement of what's about to happen really hits home

(21) Get the gear

From the moment you discover that your partner is pregnant, you'll suddenly become aware of all the 'must have' items which no self-respecting parent should do without. However, the real list of essentials might not be as long as the advertisers would have you believe.

First things first

New parenthood is big business. Scan the magazine racks, bookshops and TV channels and you'll see acre upon acre of advertising space dedicated to selling things to new mums and dads. It's easy to feel dazzled by the vast array of 'must-haves' and it's only right that you should dote on your firstborn a bit. But be realistic too. First and foremost, babies need clothes and nappies, somewhere warm to sleep, some form of flexible 'transport', and food. If you and your partner can meet these basic requirements, you'll have it covered from the start.

Ask friends who already have children what they found really useful and what, looking back now, was a waste of money. Remember, too, that you really don't need to buy everything in one go. Items such as highchairs and full-size cots can be left until later – you won't need them for a while. And bear in mind that lots of the bigger items can often be borrowed from friends or family, because no one uses tiny baby gear for long.

Limit the clothes shopping to around four or five full outfits, including something to wear outside. Your baby won't need newborn clothing for long, because babies grow so quickly, so don't buy much – if possible, get onto the nearly-new baby clothes circuit (through family and friends with older children), where the newborn clothes really are nearly new.

On the nappy front, the basic options are disposable or reusable. If you choose reusable, you'll need at least 12 and perhaps even 24 nappies to allow time to wash and dry them between uses. Babies get through six to eight nappies a day in the early weeks. You'll also need toiletries and wet wipes for changing and bathing. After battling with nappies, you'll be glad to hear that breast milk is the healthiest form of baby food – if your partner is happy to breastfeed, your life on this front is simple. If she chooses to bottle-feed, you'll need bottles, formula, sterilizing equipment and lots of practice. Your tiny consumer will also need somewhere to sleep: a crib, cot or Moses basket plus bedding (but not pillows, as they're not safe until the baby is at least a year old).

Buggies and prams

If you can't borrow a pram or buggy, buying one (even second-hand) can be a major investment for new parents, so take some time to think about what you want before hitting the shops. Agree your budget and try as many different types of pram as you can before you buy. Make sure it fits in the boot of your car (especially if it's a double buggy) and

> I can't believe how small a newborn babygrow is! #miracleoflife

test its overall size. Will it easily fit through your front door, for example? Ask yourself whether it will stand the test of time. If you are using it from birth, make sure the baby can lie completely flat, but find out if it will convert to the sitting-up type as your baby grows.

Make sure you're buying a buggy that is comfortable for you both. If possible, try to get one that is adjustable in terms of handle height, especially if you and your partner differ significantly in height or stride length. This will avoid either of you getting a bad back. If you do borrow a buggy, or buy a second-hand one, make sure that it carries the appropriate safety marks and is in good condition (preferably having been recently been serviced by a reputable dealer.)

The new baby checklist

Here's a quick rundown of the basics you'll need at, or soon after, the birth:

- 6 newborn vests (you might want to practise putting these on a teddy)
- 6 newborn babygrows
- 3 cardigans
- Scratch mitts (if the babygrows don't have 'hatches' for hands)
- Cellular or wool blankets (depending on the time of year)
- Outdoor clothing, blankets and hats
- Cot, basinette or Moses basket and bed linen
- 3 baby bottles, newborn teats, milk formula and sterilizing equiment (if your partner wants to bottle-feed)
- At least 6 muslin squares
- 1 large pack of newborn nappies (practise these on teddy too)
- Nappy sacks, or a supply of plastic bags
- Changing mat or baby dresser with a changing top
- Baby wipes
- Barrier cream for nappy rash
- Cotton wool rolls
- Unperfumed babybath suitable for washing body and hair
- Large soft towel
- Baby hair brush
- Nightlight for night-time changing and feeds (or low-wattage bulb for bedside lamp)
- Buggy, pram, or baby sling
- Baby intercom
- Car seat

Car seats

In most countries, including the UK, it is a legal requirement to ensure that all passengers in a car are secured using a seat appropriate for their height and weight. If you intend taking your baby home from hospital by car you must have a car seat for the journey and if you regularly travel by car you must invest in one. There are hundreds of options so shop around and ask other parents. Do not go for second-hand on this item.

Optional extras

Many parents buy a newborn baby carrier or sling. Apart from being really practical, everybody loves a dad with a newborn strapped to his chest. Be prepared for random women giving you admiring glances and striking up conversation. Lastly, although not really necessary at first, toys are fun for you and your baby to enjoy together.

Condensed idea
Focus on getting essential baby items first – luxuries can wait until later

(22) Practice run

As the baby's birth approaches, it's time to prepare for D-day (delivery day) itself. Talk to other dads and mums about what worked for them during labour and make sure you know how to do basic things, like understand how the new baby equipment works.

The truly 'must-have' bag

Your partner will be advised to pack a hospital bag around five weeks before her due date. Even if she is hoping to have a home birth, she'll still be advised to pack one just in case she has to make an impromptu trip to the hospital. Your midwife should also have given her an indication of the basic contents that should go into the bag. Avoid the proverbial 'kitchen sink' but, if in doubt, it's better to take things you don't use rather than miss something important.

Home birth preparations

If your partner is healthy and her pregnancy is progressing well there's every reason that she can opt for a home birth if she would like to. A few weeks before the baby's due date, the midwife will bring round a birth pack containing all the things that she will need to oversee the birth, but you'll also need to gather together the following items:

- Plastic sheeting to protect the area where you partner will give birth (usually the bed, floor or sofa), plus old towels and sheets to go on top.
- A couple of handy receptacles in case she vomits.
- A blanket or throw for her, in case she gets cold.
- Bin liners for dirty linen.

- More old sheets, towels or paper (wallpaper lining is good) for making a path between the place she will give birth and the toilet.
- Clean warm towels and a baby blanket to keep the baby warm after she's born.
- If your partner is planning on using a birth pool you'll need to borrow, hire or, if you're really committed, buy one. Ask your midwife for advice.

Don't try to improvize with any of the birth essentials

Hospital birth preparations

If your partner is planning on giving birth in hospital, visit the labour unit for a look round before the day itself. It will help to familiarize you both with the environment and allow you to practise finding your way to the department, if it's a big hospital. Take the opportunity to ask any questions you want answered.

Make a list of the phone numbers of all the people you need to ring once the baby arrives. Just as importantly, think about the order in which you're going to ring them (get this one wrong and you'll be in serious trouble). Keep the list in the hospital bag.

Make sure you've got enough change for phones and parking – start collecting it now. Mobile phones must be switched off in maternity units, so a payphone may be your next best option, especially if your less-mobile partner wants to talk too. Check out what your hospital's parking policy is; some expect you to pay several times a day, while others charge only once a day for parking and will 'exempt' you from paying again whilst accompanying someone in labour.

Pack a camera and make sure it's charged. Keep it close at hand because babies pull wonderful facial expressions in the early days. Finally, pack a pen – not just for crosswords (in the unlikely event that you're stuck for something to do), but to write down the time of birth and your baby's weight – everyone you phone will want that information.

Labour stuff for dads

Think about your own needs too as you pack the hospital bag. Dads and other birth partners sometimes pass out in maternity units because they're too hot. Labour wards are always baking, so wear layers that you can peel off. The heat can make you sleepy, and since labour can be totally exhausting, mentally and physically, the occasional nap isn't a bad idea. Bear in mind that you may have to go 24 hours or so without sleep. So doze when you can and sit down, rather than pace the floor. You might get hungry too, so pack plenty of drinks and healthy snacks, because you're unlikely to be offered much beyond a cup of tea or coffee in the maternity unit. Frozen drinks are good because they will defrost during labour but stay cool.

> 30 mins trying 2 find 'button' to collapse new buggy. More engineering than space shuttle #beatenbytech

Do the blindingly obvious

It has been known for a couple to joyfully leave the maternity unit only to return 20 minutes later to confess they couldn't work out how to secure the car seat into the car. Or for the dad to have rehearsed the route to the hospital, but to have neglected to put enough petrol in the car. Or for couples to forget to pack clothes for the new mum to return home in, not thinking that she would prefer not to wear maternity clothes. Or for dads to forget their partner's shoes. Or coat. But I'm sure it won't happen to you.

Bonus points for great home prep

- Stock up on basic things like toilet rolls and washing powder that are boring to buy but really annoying when you run out.
- Fill cupboards with pasta, tinned foods, cereals and so on – foods with long 'sell by' dates.
- Fill the freezer. During the last few weeks before the birth, make extra portions of any meals you cook and freeze them (unless you really enjoy a surprise meal, make sure you label them). Or put lots of shop-bought meals in the freezer.
- Print off address labels for baby announcement cards.
- Make a list of everyone who offers to help and their phone numbers. Making the most of extra help when you're offered it is one of the tricks of the early parenthood trade. On the whole, people enjoy being needed and will be only too pleased to help in whatever way they can. The trouble is, it's very easy to forget who said they could help, when.
- Set up a few hot meal 'deliveries' from friends for the first few days after you all return home, or just for you while you're popping backwards and forwards to the hospital.

Condensed idea
Make a list of all the practicalities surrounding the birth and how to address them

(23) D-day

You've been to the antenatal class, decorated the baby's room, bought the gear, filled the car up with petrol, and learned the breathing exercises. The freezer is loaded, the bag is packed, and you've got a list of people to call. There's really only one thing left to do.

The final countdown

First of all, don't think of that due date as fixed – babies rarely come exactly on time. By the time yours does it could be as much as two weeks past your partner's due date. Different couples approach this 'overdue' time in different ways: some clear their diaries from the due

If your partner has been practising yoga during pregnancy, she'll find the exercise especially soothing and helpful now

date onwards in readiness for the big event, while others go into social overdrive. On balance it's probably better to keep your social life going for a while so that if the baby does come late, your partner won't be sitting twiddling her thumbs. This might be a good time to suggest a little pampering to make her feel better about herself and help her relax. And make sure she always has your contact number.

Under ideal circumstances, labour begins naturally, but if the dates start dragging, be prepared for a parade of suggestions from just about everybody for jump-starting the process with a variety of techniques. Exercise, hot curries, castor oil, raspberry leaf tea, pineapple and, of course, sex may all feature (with varied levels of scientific backing) so have fun trying them out, but don't try anything too outrageous without checking with your doctor that it's safe.

Signs of labour

When the time finally comes, you're unlikely to mistake the signs of labour, but the golden rule is always to contact the midwife if you are in any doubt. The main indication is likely to be longer, increasingly stronger and more regular contractions (as opposed to same-strength, infrequent Braxton Hicks). These may also be accompanied by backache, nausea, an upset stomach or your partner having the urge to go to the toilet as the baby's head presses on her bowel. Your partner may have a 'show', which is when the plug of sticky pink mucus which has sealed the womb during pregnancy comes out of the vagina. She shouldn't lose a lot of blood with a show so if she does, telephone the midwife straightaway.

Your partner's waters may also break as the bag of water surrounding the baby (the amniotic sac) gives way. Waters break with either a trickle or a gush, but once it happens, you should phone the midwife or hospital to let them know. She'll probably be advised to go straight to the hospital. If she has opted for a home birth, follow the procedure you have agreed with your midwife about the onset of labour.

Types of pain pelief during labour

Your partner will probably want to choose
from among the following types of pain relief:

- **Self-help.** Relaxation and breathing
  techniques are a good start, as is keeping
  mobile and taking back massages from you.
- **Gas and air (Entenox).** This mixture of
  oxygen and nitrous oxide is breathed in
  through a mouthpiece, normally as a contraction begins. It makes
  some women feel sick, sleepy or lightheaded, but also makes the
  pain easier to bear.
- **TENS.** This is a small machine that is taped to your partner's
  back to deliver small electrical impulses which stimulate natural
  endorphins (body chemicals that lessen pain). Try renting one
  before D-day so your partner can experiment with it.
- **Injections.** Some women opt for an intramuscular injection of
  a pain-relieving drug (normally pethidine). It takes 20 minutes
  to work and it lasts for about two hours.
- **Epidural anaesthesia.** This is a type of local anaesthetic,
  injected through a very thin tube into the space between
  the bones of your partner's spine. The anaesthetic is then
  pumped in continuously or topped up as required. It is highly
  effective but there are disadvantages too; talk to your midwife
  beforehand so you know exactly what these are. A spinal is
  similar to an epidural but is administered in a one-off dose,
  rather than topped up. It may be given if there is not enough
  time to administer an epidural.
- **Alternative therapies.** These include acupuncture,
  aromatherapy, homeopathy, hypnosis or reflexology.

Try not to panic when contractions start or when your partner's waters break – this is exactly the time she will need you to be strong for her. Stay calm and focus on her. Help her relax by helping her breathe, massaging her back and by using other relaxation techniques you've agreed beforehand. If her contractions have started but her waters have not broken, the healthcare team may suggest that you wait until they are coming more regularly – perhaps five minutes apart and lasting for between 30 seconds and a minute. If, however, you sense your partner would like to be in hospital now, say so. When labour begins in earnest, knowing already what your partner wants will help you to support her better,

> Thunderbirds are go! It's really starting. See you on the other side. #soontobedad

so make sure this is in the birth plan. If she's having difficulties, it may be down to you to speak on her behalf. If the route to hospital is busy or long, leave sooner rather than later. Call the hospital before you leave to let them know you are coming and make sure that your partner has her bag and, if she carries them, her pregnancy notes. When you arrive at the hospital, your partner will be admitted to the labour ward.

Becoming a mum, becoming a dad

However labour proceeds, your role as an attendant first-time father is the same: to keep your partner company, hold her hand, wipe her face and tell her that she's amazing. To breathe along with her and support her decisions as the labour proceeds. Finally and wonderfully, to sit alongside her when you both meet your son or daughter for the first time.

Condensed idea
You're the support team – she's in charge

(24) Labour stages

If you're able to be at the birth, you have a vital role to play as an engaged, composed, positive and encouraging presence, talking with and listening calmly to your partner and the health professionals, even if you're actually feeling pretty anxious inside.

The first stage

If your partner plans to have the baby in hospital but goes there before labour is established, she may be given the option of going home again for a while. She will be considered to be in 'established labour' once her contractions have caused her cervix to become at least 4 cm (1½ in) dilated, or open, but it can take many hours before it is fully dilated (10 cm/4 in). If she opts to go home, encourage her to try eating or drinking something even if she's not especially hungry or thirsty, because it will give her energy. As her contractions get stronger and more painful during this early labour stage, encourage her to keep gently active, because it will help the baby move down into her pelvis. A warm shower or bath at this point will help to ease her pain. Offer to rub her back, because this may help too.

> Apologies to @Jane, but it's about now that perhaps I'm feeling a little too thankful that I'm a man. #justtellingitlikeitis

Once labour is established, the midwife will check your partner's progress regularly. She will tell your partner not to push at this stage, as she must wait until the cervix is fully open. Breathing exercises can help her to overcome this urge and your partner might find it helps if you do them with her. The midwife will monitor your baby's heart throughout labour because this indicates how well the baby is coping with the process. If your partner's labour is slower than expected (normally if her contractions are not frequent or strong enough), the midwife or doctor may recommend trying a couple of things to get things moving. They may break your partner's waters through a painless procedure using an amniohook (a 'crochet hook' type implement), or, if this doesn't work, they may give her an oxytocin drip to encourage contractions.

The second stage

This stage begins when your partner's cervix is fully dilated and lasts until the birth of the baby. This is the stage of labour when your partner may feel panicked, want to go home, change her mind about having a baby, or become incredibly focused and 'in her own world'. It's the time when you should draw on all your powers to support her. Offer to hold her hand, wipe her face with a cool cloth, give her sips of water, or follow

Assisted delivery and caesareans

Some women require assistance when giving birth, especially if the baby shows signs of distress, is in an awkward position or if your partner is exhausted. There are three main types of intervention that may be used:

- **Ventouse.** This involves using an instrument that uses suction to pull the baby out. A plastic or metal cup is fitted firmly onto the baby's head and attached to a suction device. Timed with contractions and your partner's pushing, the obstetrician or midwife pulls to help deliver the baby. It can leave a bruise on the baby's head.
- **Forceps.** These are smooth metal instruments that look like large salad serving spoons and they are designed to fit round a baby's head. Like ventouse, they are used in time with the mother's contractions. Forceps can leave marks on your baby's face but these will quickly fade.
- **Caesarean section.** This is a surgical operation where the baby is delivered through the abdomen, either for emergency reasons or because the health professionals decide in advance that labour may be dangerous for mum or baby. A caesarean section involves major surgery and usually uses epidural or spinal anaesthesia, so mum is awake throughout. The cut is usually made just below the bikini line, and there is no pain, just abdominal tugging and pulling. It takes up to 10 minutes to deliver the baby and 40 minutes for the whole operation. A screen will separate you from the action, but you can be present throughout.

her instruction to 'shut the hell up' – anything she wants. It's important that she finds a position that she prefers and that will make labour easier for her, whether this is standing, sitting, kneeling, squatting, lying propped up in bed or on her side, so offer to help her move. Help your partner to hear the midwife's instructions – whether to breathe, wait or push. The baby's head will usually emerge first. This is known as 'crowning' and you may want to look but, equally, you may not. After a couple more contractions his head will be born, usually facing towards your partner's back. His head will then turn sideways and then the rest of his body will be fully born. All being well, your partner can have the baby lifted straight onto her before the cord is cut by your midwife or – if you would like to – by you. Some babies need mucus to be cleared out of their noses and mouths, or they need to be taken off for extra help to get their breathing established, but whatever happens, they will not be kept away from you any longer than necessary.

The third stage

This stage involves a few more contractions which push out the placenta. This is sometimes speeded along by an injection of syntocinon, which also helps prevent heavy bleeding. It's possible that your partner will need stitches after childbirth, although small tears are often left to heal without them. You will also be offered an injection of Vitamin K for your baby, which your midwife should have talked to you about beforehand, and then he'll be weighed and measured. The biggest surprise? If you've been talking to your baby, he'll recognize the sound of your voice, so he'll ike being close to you – his mum and dad – just after the birth. Your first child will then be given a band with your name on it, and many people treasure this tiny piece of plastic for the rest of their lives.

Condensed idea
Forewarned is forearmed: get to know what happens in the four stages of labour

25 A life less ordinary

Occasionally, a baby needs extra care in hospital, sometimes in a specialist neonatal unit. Having a baby in special care is an anxious time for any parent but dads, in particular, can feel torn in every direction. Make sure you look after your partner and yourself.

Premature and special care babies

Most babies are born between weeks 39 and 41 of the pregnancy. If a baby is born before the 37th completed week, it is said to be pre-term or premature. Very early babies (those born as much as 10 or more weeks early) often need lots of medical intervention to help them survive the first few weeks of life. They are likely to go into a Special Care Baby Unit (SCBU, or 'scaboo'), a High Dependency Unit (HDU) or even the Neonatal Intensive Care Unit (NICU). However, any baby, born at any gestation, may be placed in special care if he has breathing difficulties or feeding problems.

> Elated at his arrival, but worried and anxious too. The doctors and midwives are amazing but we just want him home. #lifeinSCBU

When they visit hospital maternity departments before the birth, many couples opt not to see the special care units. They don't want to tempt fate, thinking that if they don't go there, the baby won't either. The truth is, however, that even though only a relatively small proportion of babies will need specialist neonatal care, parents will be better equipped to deal with it if they have some feel for what the specialist environment looks like. So make a point of visiting the unit before your baby is born, just in case. Get the staff to talk you through the equipment; ask them what each machine, tube or device does. It's also good to prepare yourself (as best you can) for how small a premature baby can be. Many new parents think an 3.5 kg (8 lb) baby is tiny, so if your baby is under 2 kg (4 lb) he really will be very little indeed. Remind yourself that even relatively 'large' premature babies look tiny when surrounded by all the equipment used in a neonatal unit.

Daily life in special care

No one enjoys having their newborn baby ensconced in a neonatal unit and it is natural to feel extremely anxious. Mums and dads with special care babies aren't always able to get close to them, or cuddle them very much, if at all, and this adds to an emotionally draining experience. There will be ways that you can interact with him, however, and it's very important that you do – he's your baby and he needs you. Talk to your team of health professionals about what is and isn't possible, and be creative.

Be prepared to experience a wide range of emotions and don't worry about how you 'should' be feeling. If your baby needs to stay in neonatal care for a relatively short time after the birth, your partner may stay in hospital with him. This poses particular challenges for dads: adjusting to the new role of 'father', dealing with the worry of a baby in special care, and looking after a partner who is recovering from labour. In turn, you may spend a lot of time on your own, racing around, pretty much yo-yoing in and out of the hospital. It's easy to feel exhausted, lonely and anxious. Many men also feel guilty about not being able to be at the hospital all the time. Be aware of your feelings, but remember something else too: although your baby's stay in hospital feels like a crisis to you both, you now have a child – so make sure you celebrate his arrival in the world too.

The specialist care team

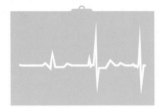

All specialist staff in neonatal units will be committed to keeping your partner and you at the very centre of your baby's care. The most enlightened units consider parents not to be visitors, but a vital part of the team caring for your baby. Take time to ask hospital staff the following and write down the answers so that you don't have to remember them during a crisis. Find out:

- Who is in charge and who to contact with questions.
- Who would be on your team, from doctors to social workers.
- What their schedules are and the times that shifts change.
- When the care team gets together to discuss a case.
- How you would be updated if there were any changes in the baby's condition or decisions to be made.
- What types of equipment and tests might be used.
- What you would be able to do to help and to interact with your baby.
- Where you can purchase food and eat.
- Where phones and computers are located.
- What support groups and spiritual services are on hand.

Others are there to help

You might be the type of person who normally hesitates to ask for help, but now is not the time to be macho. You owe it to your baby and your partner to get supported yourself so you can better support them. However difficult it seems to switch your brain off, try to get enough sleep, even if this means asking someone else to stay with the baby for a couple of hours. Ask friends and family to provide meals for you too; it will help you keep your strength up and maintain some sense of normality.

If you work, talk to your employer about your circumstances as early as you can. Some dads say they found it helpful to go to work a bit while the baby was in hospital and then take their full entitlement once the baby was at home. On the other hand, your partner is likely to really need your support at this time, so weigh things up. Take lots of photos every day and celebrate those developmental milestones. Babies change daily, and everyone will want to see pictures, especially those who can't visit.

Trusting each other

Sometimes, a new mum may be discharged from hospital before her baby. This can be tough – probably the last thing any mum or dad expects is to go home without their precious baby. If this happens, make it a priority to look after each other. Spend time with your partner, both with and apart from the baby, safe in the knowledge that your baby will be receiving all the care he needs. Even in this anxious time, work as a team and allow each other enough time to rest and physically recover from the birth. Respect each other's feelings and make decisions together.

Condensed idea
If your baby requires specialist care, make sure you look after yourself and your partner too

26 New skills

There is a tendency for brand new parents to feel that they should know all about every aspect of baby care from day one. But like most things, the skills of looking after a baby need to be learned and it may take a little time to get the hang of how to do everything.

Where's the manual?

It's often said that men don't read instructions. We roll our eyes in a 'not that old chestnut' kind of way when we hear someone say it, but then we discover that the flat-packed piece of furniture we have been assembling hasn't quite turned out like it showed in the picture. If this stirs even the faintest bit of recognition in you, I've got some great news – babies don't come with instructions. There's absolutely nothing that you positively have to read. Even books like this can only go so far – because this is your baby, your parenthood and your baby's personality.

> First nappy change successfully negotiated. Bring it on! Time to take my rightful place in the pantheon of new dads. #roundofapplause

Before becoming a dad yourself you may have had very little contact with other people's babies; perhaps none at all. The same may be true for your partner too and so the sense of nervousness at having to handle and care for a very small baby, even your own, is perfectly natural. You wouldn't expect to be able to drive a car from the first time you sat in it, so don't expect to do this perfectly to begin with either.

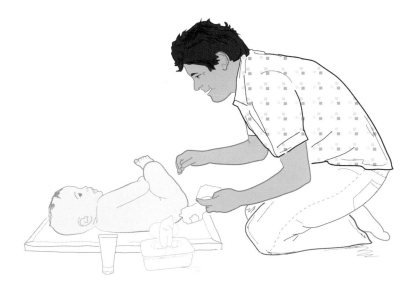

Inevitably, new mums tend to take the lead in looking after your little one, but make sure you get involved with baby care during the early days too. Contrary to how you might feel, the baby's head will absolutely not fall off when you pick up him up, neither will her leg come off in your big hands whilst changing her nappy. What you will find, however and in common with every parent, are times when you put nappies and babygrows on back to front, inside out, upside down. He'll wee all over the changing mat (or himself, or you, or someone else) just as you've laid the dry stuff out, or she'll be sick over your shoulder and herself as soon as you've changed her, but this is just the stuff of learning to be a parent. Get stuck in with cuddling, changing and bathing as soon as you can. Before you know it, your feelings of inadequacy will soon subside. Your confidence will grow in leaps and bounds and you'll find yourself having fun as you build your relationship with your new son or daughter.

Breasts or bottles?

One of the first skills that your partner (and you) will have to get to grips with is that of feeding – whether breastfeeding or bottle-feeding. Your partner will probably have decided her preference long before the

The benefits of breastfeeding

Breastfeeding mums are often thrilled to find out that they will naturally use up to 500 calories a day. They also have a lower risk of developing breast and ovarian cancer than women who haven't breastfed. But there are more benefits too:

- Breastfeeding protects your baby from infections and diseases.
- Breast milk costs nothing.
- Breast milk is (almost literally) on tap whenever your baby needs a feed, assuming your partner is around.
- Breast milk is always the right temperature.
- Breastfeeding helps to build a strong bond between mother and baby.
- Breastfeeding takes work and practice, but it will build your partner's confidence in herself as a mother.
- Breastfed babies have less chance of being constipated, suffering diarrhoea or vomiting.
- Breastfed babies are less likely to develop eczema.
- Breastfed babies have fewer chest and ear infections.
- Breastfed babies are less likely to become obese, with the additional difficulties this brings later in life.

baby was born and it's important that she feels supported by you in the choices that she makes. Breastfeeding is the healthiest way to feed a baby (see box) and breast milk alone is recommended for around the first six months of your baby's life. After that, giving her breast milk alongside other food will help her continue to grow and develop.

Obviously, as a man you may feel more useful if your partner opts for bottle feeding, but if your partner breastfeeds she will need considerable support from you as she learns this new skill for herself. Help her get comfortable for feeding, reassure her that she's doing a great job and offer her something to eat or drink as she feeds the baby. Later on you could think about feeding your baby yourself from a bottle containing your partner's breast milk.

Many men, while recognizing the value of breastfeeding, find it slightly hard to adjust to the idea that parts of their partner's body which they previously considered their own personal playthings are now used in a much more 'functional' capacity. It's okay to feel a little left out – even a twinge of jealousy from time to time – but you'll have them back again soon enough and in the meantime and when your partner's ready to, you can enjoy her breasts' more ample proportions!

Bottle-feeding basics

If your partner chooses to bottle-feed, encourage her to ask for help during the initial feeds. Many new mums who aren't breastfeeding seem reluctant to ask for help but just like breastfeeding mums, they need help and guidance. And in this case it's never too soon for you to get stuck in. Always use sterilized equipment and make up your baby's feeds exactly according to the manufacturer's instructions – never add a little extra or take a little out. If you lose count of the scoops you have put in, discard the bottle and start again. Never heat a baby's milk in the microwave because it can cause hot spots in the fluid that can burn your baby's mouth. And if in doubt, ask! Midwives, doctors, family and friends will want to help you gain confidence in handling your child.

condensed idea
Learning to care for a new baby takes time, so relax and enjoy the ride

27 The first 24 hours

There's something magical about the first time that your baby looks you in the eye or grips your finger. It's not unusual, however, for these feelings of wonderment to be accompanied by a growing sense of incredulity. How can someone so small demand so much time?

Recovering from labour

Returning home from the hospital, or restoring the house back to normal after a home birth, marks the beginning of a period of adjustment to this new way of living, as a family of three. The first thing to be aware of is that even the most straightforward of births can leave a new mum feeling shell-shocked; whoever coined the term 'labour' knew what they were talking about. Despite these feelings of exhaustion, however, it is not uncommon for mums to have a sudden burst of energy again once the baby is born. This won't last for long, though, and so it may fall to you to help your partner manage her energy levels during the early days and help out more when she needs some vital rest.

> What on earth did we do before we had kids? #busydad

At the same time, chances are that you also found labour mentally and emotionally exhausting. Apart from the tiredness that invariably results from supporting your partner and, perhaps, witnessing the birth, there's the mixture of elation and trepidation that comes with the earliest hours of parenthood. So try to disregard any impulse to get things 'sorted out' – the feeling is only natural but it's important that you give yourself a bit of time to stop, recover and rest.

Is your baby a sleeper?

Research in the 1990s defined three (perhaps a little unsubtle) baby 'types' in order to help parents respond to the very individual needs of their child in the early days. An 'average baby' sleeps 12–20 hours a day and feeds 6–14 times. When awake, he is usually quiet, listens to the noises around him and enjoys being handled. If unhappy he will try and console himself. An 'easy baby' sleeps for longer stretches, feeds 6–14 times a day and is generally very easy to please. A 'placid baby' sleeps 18–20 hours a day and may only feed 4–6 times a day. When awake he is calm and placid, making few demands for attention.

Surviving the early days

While these are busy times, recognize that these days are also really precious. As anyone further down the road of parenthood will tell you, they pass very quickly indeed, so take time to savour special moments.

- Everyone takes a while to adjust after the birth and to their new roles, so give yourself a bit of time: don't try to cram in too much activity or expect to know how to do everything.
- Work smarter, not always harder, by prioritizing: think about what you can leave for another day and what you should do straight away.
- Manage the flow of visitors, but when they come, ask them to help you, rather than you helping them.
- First and foremost be alert to your partner's needs as she adjusts to becoming a new mum.

Whichever 'type' of baby you eventually experience, a typical 24-hour period will see your new baby busying himself with four handy activities: sleeping, feeding, pooing/weeing and crying. Fortunately these mostly come in descending order of frequency. While you may be elated at your new arrival, there's no getting away from the fact that caring for babies is a time-consuming, dirty and often mundane business. If you formerly had a carefree life with few responsibilities, where the weekends and evenings left you free to do as you like, it can take a considerable adjustment to deal with the constant demands of a new baby.

Planning it out

Antenatal teachers often employ a useful device to help soon-to-be parents to consider the energy demands of a new baby. Draw a clock face with 24 hours on it to represent your average day, then shade in areas to represent the main things you do, when you do them and the time it takes to get them done. Include the things that you have to do for everyday life, such as food shopping, cleaning, doing the laundry and so on. Then comes the tricky bit: add the baby's likely demands for the same 24-hour period to your clock face. How does this fit in with your own expectations for the time that's going to be available to you? It's by no means an exact science but many expectant mums and dads find it a practical way to think and talk about these time issues.

> 2am. Up again. Feed and nappy change. Whoever invented the phrase 'sleeping like a baby'? #nocturnalparent

Busy but thinking

Although your partner will probably assume the role and responsibilities of a main carer in the first few days, getting to grips with feeding and recovery after labour, most dads find themselves assuming the role

of 'multi-tasking male' (or 'working prototype' as I saw on a T-shirt recently). If your partner has remained in hospital for a while, there's plenty of racing around to be done, ringing and texting family and friends, posting the all-important photos online, getting your home back in order, remembering to eat and generally going to and fro between hospital and home. Even with a home birth, the same can be true – chores to be done, shopping to be bought, visitors to be coordinated. Amidst all this, be aware of the challenges your partner is facing as she adjusts to new motherhood. Ask her gently how you can help – don't always assume that you know. Above all, try to get some perspective. The list of things for you to learn can seem enormous, but rest assured, within a few weeks you'll wonder what all the fuss was about.

Condensed idea
Don't underestimate the adjustment that is required for a newborn baby's timetable

(28) Jump in

Nothing can completely prepare you for the moment that the two of you are left on your own for the first time as new parents, literally holding the baby. As the front door clicks shut your first thought might be 'Help! What do we do now?' Don't panic, just jump right in.

Don't hold back

All of us learn in different ways – visually, logically, on our own or talking things over with other people – but whatever your learning style, we all learn much more through doing than by any other method. You can only read so many books, watch so many movies, and talk to so many experts about learning to swim – one day you just have to get into the pool. Similarly, the best way to learn how to be a great dad is by doing it: tackle those everyday challenges like bathing the baby and changing nappies. In the early days, it can be tempting to hang back and allow your partner to take the lion's share of the childcare. You might rationalize this by saying that your role will kick in much later on – when your daughter can do more, communicate more and be generally more, well, interesting. The truth is, however, that the sooner you engage with your new daughter the sooner she – and you – will reap the benefits.

Getting ready for a bath

It really doesn't matter what time of day you bath your baby. If you're a working dad, evening bathing may fit better into your lifestyle, so you might want to mention this to your partner. In general, however, giving your baby a bath before a feed is usually better than after (would you

The other end

The colours of your baby's poo will change from day to day after birth, from thick black meconium, through green, to an eventual mustard colour. It may not be much of a conversation starter, but the colour acts as  a good indicator of your child's general health, so keep an eye on it. Occasionally, new parents are alarmed to see what appears to be blood in their baby's nappy. The reddish tinge can be due to several things but, most commonly, it's caused by substances (urates) in urine which react with the chemicals in a disposable nappy's stay-dry lining. It causes the baby no discomfort and goes quickly, but if you're concerned, talk to your midwife. Apart from a little petroleum jelly to help ease off sticky meconium, avoid using nappy cream early on because it can prevent the stay-dry nappy lining from working effectively, actually keeping liquid in contact with the skin.

want to go swimming after a large milky meal?). It will also help her to sleep well. Most young babies don't actually like bathtime to begin with, but soon learn to love it. Before you begin, make sure you have everything you need (a sponge or flannel, a clean towel, a nappy and baby clothes) nearby. You don't need to spend a fortune on baby bath products; water alone is fine, unless you've taken off a soiled nappy, in which case use a simple baby soap. Leave your phone on voicemail so you're not distracted. Wash your hands, then fill the bath with about 13 cm (5 in) of water. Check the temperature by dipping your elbow or wrist into the water; it should be warm, but not hot.

In she goes!

Undress your baby and wrap her in a towel. Newbie dads can find wet, slippery babies hard to handle, so you might want to clean her face and hair now, before giving her a bath. Dip a piece of cotton wool into the warm water, and gently wipe it across one eye, starting near her nose and moving outward. Then use a new piece of cotton wool for her other eye. Newborn babies are particularly prone to mild eye infections; if she's showing signs of this, tip the two cotton wool pieces for her eyes into cooled, boiled water from a separate bowl. You'll need two pieces of clean, dampened cotton wool to wipe behind each of her ears, and another piece for her neck creases. Yes, you're getting through an insane amount of cotton wool on one bath, but go with it.

You can clean her head by holding her over the bath and gently washing her head with a sponge. Then comes the big moment. Unwrap the towel, and gently lower her into the bath, feet first, using one hand to support her neck and head. Use your other hand to wipe over her body with a sponge or flannel, moving from her neck to her toes. Once you're an experienced baby bather, you can boost your baby's confidence by gently 'bouncing' her in the water and letting her kick against the side of the bowl, bath or sink. It will help to give her a sense of stability and feel she is in a safe place. At all times remember the number one rule of bathtime: never leave your baby unattended in the bath, even for a moment. When she's clean and has had enough, lift her out by keeping one hand behind her head and neck, and the other under her bottom. Then wrap her in a warm towel and enjoy a quiet cuddle before dressing her. Initially, bathing may be a two-person operation, with either you or your partner in the bath and the other handing your baby in and then taking her out again to dry her.

> Woah! Bathtime is kind of scary, kind of fun. She's a slippery little fish! #firsttimeparentseh?

How to change a nappy

Newborn babies, especially breast-fed ones, wee and poo a lot. Really, an astonishing amount. Luckily, nappy changing is fairly technical and comes with rules. If you have baby girl, always clean her bottom by washing from front to back. This prevents bacteria from the anus (back passage) getting into the vagina. If you have a baby boy, have a tissue ready to place strategically as soon as you remove his nappy as early on baby boys have an instant reflex to wee as soon as their penis is uncovered. To save yourself from ending up, weirdly, with wet baby clothes but a dry nappy, always make sure a baby boy's penis is pointing down when putting his nappy on. Take care to clean any skin which has had urine or faeces on it – especially all the folds of skin.

Condensed idea
Changing nappies and giving baths are a great way to get to know your baby

29 Love at first sight?

Contrary to conventional wisdom, not every mum or dad instantly falls in love with their new baby. It's nothing to feel guilty about – as you get involved with bathing, changing, cuddling and being with your baby, you'll soon see this relationship begin to develop.

Not quite what you were expecting

Babies are a miracle. Most dads would say, without irony, that they would die for their kids in a heartbeat. We actually ache with love for our sons or daughters. When they are first born, however, the romantic notion of loving their baby at first sight is, for many fathers, exactly that – a fictional concept with little basis in real life. If you can get them to set aside their rose-tinted spectacles for a moment, most dads (and many mums) will admit that when they first caught a glimpse of their brand new baby they didn't instantly adore him; it took a little time. In fact, the average new dad reports that it takes at least a month or two, perhaps more, to feel a real connection with their firstborn child.

> I can't decide whether he looks more like Winston Churchill or Mao Zedong. With respect to them both, things can only get better. #goodlookingboy

Considering what they've been through, it's unsurprising that few newborns would win a beauty contest when they first appear. Cone-shaped heads, red wrinkled skin, puffy faces and enlarged genitals are

par for the course. Many parents confess, a few years on, that their baby was not quite what they expected and the same may happen to you. It could be that you secretly thought (and even hoped) that he would be a girl (or vice versa), you're shocked by how he looks, or you're disappointed that he doesn't look more like you.

New mums and dads are often racked with guilt as they experience these feelings for themselves, not realizing that, to a certain extent, it's pretty normal. Even if your partner is totally besotted from the start, there's no need to feel guilty or ashamed if you don't feel the same way yourself. Building a relationship with anyone takes time. Commit to working at it from the very beginning by pitching in with the baby care – the nappy changing, the rocking, the burping, and, of course, the bathing. It's practical, fun and also the perfect 'brownie point' earner. Try saying 'No, you have a rest darling' (while we're off to the bathroom for some fun). The more you get involved with the day-to-day care of your baby, you'll find, like most dads, that your love for him grows as your relationship with him develops. It may take a little while, but eventually you'll look back and wonder how you ever got by without him.

Eight ways to build a better bond

- Give her lots of skin-to-skin contact – this applies to new dads just as much as new mums.
- Sing to your baby – choose a catchy but diabolical chart topper or an ancient folk song; it doesn't matter.
- Take a bath together – remember the bath will have to be at baby friendly temperature (i.e. slightly cool for you).
- If the baby feeds but doesn't settle, make sure you're the one walking her around, not your partner.
- Talk to your baby, quietly, when it's just the two of you, with no one else around and no distractions.
- Watch your baby as she sleeps.
- Keep a journal of the things that come to mind as you adjust to fatherhood during the first few weeks. When you look back, you'll realize the impact that your child had on you.
- Buy that remote control car if you want – your baby can't play with it yet, but one day soon you'll be able to play together.

What if I missed the birth?

Many dads are present at the birth of their child. Some fathers, however, miss it, through no fault of their own. Working abroad or away from home can leave new dads with little chance of getting to the birth, but some dads just get stuck in traffic jams, train delays, or a myriad of other things. If you fully expected to be at the birth of your child but just couldn't make it, you'll understandably be pretty fed up. You may even wonder whether it will have any sort of long-term impact on your relationship with your partner or your ability to bond with your new baby. But while it might take a bit of time to work through with your partner, because she probably wanted you to be there even more than you did yourself, the damage isn't as great as you probably think. There's no reason why missing the birth should have any long-term implications for your relationship with your child, unless you continue to worry about it. So let go of any guilt and get stuck in when you do get there.

Although it can be difficult in the early days, try to carve out some time to talk to each other about how you feel and what, if anything, you're finding difficult. It's easy to misread behaviour: dads who appear uninterested may really be feeling nervous and inadequate about handling a small baby. Likewise, mums who appear totally enthralled about junior may secretly feel overwhelmed by the responsibility. Don't assume that you know what's going on – find time to check how she feels and express your own thoughts and emotions.

Newborn interaction

In the first month or two a baby won't do much more than sleep, eat, poo and cry, which at first glance doesn't seem the best foundation for a lifelong loving relationship. You'll find it easier to build a rapport once you're able to elicit some kind of response from your child, rather than just watching him sleep and feed all day. If you really want to get a reaction, take a more deliberate step towards interaction. Look into your baby's face and deliberately stick your tongue out, waiting to see if he copies you (don't worry, though, if he doesn't immediately), or place your finger onto the palm of his hand and let him grasp hold of it. If you stroke his cheek, his head will turn, as if he is looking to feed from the breast.

Condensed idea
Don't worry if it's not love at first sight – get involved, and the feeling will come

30 Gadgets and gizmos

Now we're talking. If ever there was a domain where the new dad can consider himself king, the world of toys and labour-saving gadgets must be it. But how do you tell the difference between an enticing but passing fad item and one that will stand the test of time?

Go on, you know you want to

Many a new dad has been known to rush out immediately to buy the latest remote-control car racing track for his baby, to perfectly complement the games console that he's already purchased (for 'research' purposes). And it's not just toys you'll be drawn to buying – that's just the tip of the iceberg. With life-saving devices here, essential gadgets there, becoming a parent opens you up to a myriad of opportunities to spend money. The advertising is mind-bogglingly sophisticated – even your social network page will begin to promote products to you as soon as you use it to reveal you're going to be a dad.

The urge to 'invest' can be huge. You want to give your child the best start you can – and it's absolutely right that you should – but it's easy to get drawn into spending money on things you soon discover you didn't need, didn't really want and definitely couldn't afford. Plus the potential for clutter is amazing. If you've ever visited a friend and tripped over the baby walker, bouncer and baby gym before landing finally on the huge plastic hippo in the living room, you'll know what I mean. One friend of mine gave one-week-old our son a Welsh rugby shirt (replaced with an English one by me immediately, of course). When he had kids, I happily gave him a similarly useless present – all the 'labour-saving devices' and gadgets that we had once thought we desperately needed.

Worth the investment

Earlier chapters looked at the things you definitely do need to get hold of in readiness for the arrival of your baby (see pages 84–87). Beyond those essentials (clothing and nappies), it's worth investing in a buggy, a good mattress and, if relevant, a car seat. The main thing here is to be practical and talk to other mums and dads about what works for them.

Kick the gadget habit

Make sure you're controlling the gadgets, rather than them controlling you. Here's some tips for dealing with the overwhelming number of products:

- Recognize that there are some amazing devices available to new dads and mums. Use your common sense to decide which are really useful and which you can do without.
- Encourage people to give you the receipt for presents. Early on, people are used to presents doubling up and don't mind too much if you decide to exchange their gift for something else.
- Keep the packaging for a while. You can resell items that you haven't used very much but can't take back to the shop.
- Be generous. If you've got too much stuff, consider giving things away, contributing to the new-parent 'second-hand economy'.
- Learn from your mistakes. Beware the 'wet wipe warmer'. This is a genuine product. Need I say more?
- Remember that although there are lots of things you can buy to engage your baby even from an early stage, that nothing will engage her better than you.

Take the buggy for example. It's all very well to have bought the latest three-wheeled, supercruiser iWhizz, but if you can't pack it down with one hand to throw it in the boot of the car or haul onto a bus – while balancing your baby on your hip – forget it.

To monitor or not to monitor?

One big category for gadgetry overspend is the baby monitor. Don't get me wrong, a good baby monitor is a great idea and certainly should have its place on your must-have list. The challenge is the seemingly endless technological options: remote-control cameras, video, temperature gauges, heart and movement monitors and transmitters so powerful they can confuse satellite systems. Bear in mind that cleverer doesn't always mean better. Be wary of purchasing any clever device (baby monitor or not) that

> Just found greatest gadget. Makes tea, feeds baby, does dishes. Yes, ladies, it's called a husband. Pricey though. #ImaMarketersDream

lulls you into a false sense of security by removing your need to use your common sense ('I can switch off because the machine will tell me if something's wrong'). Also, ask yourself whether a baby monitor that offers a video image of your sleeping cherub will really lessen your desire to go and check. Interestingly, some parents report that devices like this actually make them more anxious.

Keep an eye on the cash

It's very easy to get into debt before you become a parent. Once the baby arrives, it's even easier. A quick Internet search reveals how common a problem this is, with many organizations offering advice and tips for parents who have found themselves with bills too big to pay. Beware, in particular, the impulse purchase. In the age of the Internet, 'harmless' browsing can prove to be an expensive business: it's even got its own

term: WILFing (as in 'What Am I Looking For?'), where there's only a momentary click between seeing and purchasing. If you know you have a habit of overspending, consider reducing the number of credit cards you hold, working on more of a cash basis instead of running up credit.

Keep it simple

Rediscovering the simpler things in life can be a great early lesson to learn as you get ready to be a dad. If you haven't yet been to a first birthday party filled with lavish presents for a baby who is actually much more fascinated by the cardboard box one of them came in, chances are that you will before long. Most of all, steer away from products that, perhaps obliquely, offer to do your job for you. Even from a few weeks of age, your daughter will opt for you sitting and reading her a book, over a beeping, flashing machine every time.

Condensed idea
Some gadgets are undoubtedly clever, but think carefully about what you really need

(31) Crowd control

As soon as the baby arrives, doting grandparents, brand new aunts and uncles, supportive friends and inquisitive neighbours will all want a peek at the new arrival. It's great to know that people are keen to be involved, but it's also good to know how to manage them.

Visitors, visitors, everywhere

For a new dad, showing off your new baby is a fantastic experience. Oohs and aaahhs, hugs and kisses, pats on the back and manly handshakes all round. Quite rightly, you'll probably be as keen as anyone to show off your new offspring, but you'll find entertaining visitors can be tiring too, especially as your partner is trying to recover from labour and you're both getting to grips with your new roles as mum and dad. You need to strike a balance so that you can look after your partner, your baby and yourself without the danger of offending anyone.

With your partner understandably immersed in the practicalities of recovery and brand new motherhood, managing the flow of visitors is an important role for any new dad. Your priority is your partner, your baby and, for now, yourself – you're a new group that needs protecting while you

My father-in-law just put his mug on a breast pad. He thought it was a drinks mat. #Imnottellinghim

find your feet. Also, small babies can become fractious if constantly handed from person to person; don't forget they've only just met you, never mind anyone else.

You've called her WHAT?

Few things cause as much disagreement amongst family and friends as the subject of names. It is amazing how many couples are devastated by the response to their name for a baby. A long silence, followed by 'Mmmmm... well it's unusual...'

It's all a matter of taste, really. You may think that Lady Gaga is the most beautiful, perfect name for your new little poppet but, unfortunately, not everyone else will. The fashion in names changes constantly: you don't meet too many young Dereks and Clives any more, but who knows when they might come back?

Some families expect children to pass down 'family' names into the next generation. Your dilemma may revolve around family expectation versus your freedom to choose any name you want. For some new mums and dads, it's simply not a problem; for others, it's worth a fight. Some keep the peace by burying the name within a list of others, while others take the bull by the horns and resist it altogether.

Whatever your feelings regarding names, prepare for a range of opinions. You simply can't please all of the people all of the time, so choose names that you, as parents, feel happy with. Be sensitive, but if you really don't want your baby named after some distant elderly relative, make it clear right from the start. It is your choice and only yours. They'll get over it (eventually!).

Hospital visitors

If your partner is in hospital, you'll find that maternity units are adept at controlling visitor numbers. They normally have quite strict visitor policies, typically accepting only two visitors at any one time, plus you, and often no children under 14 unless they are a brother or sister. Set your own ground rules too. Err on the regimented side about the number of visitors and the length of time they stay. Most people will understand. If you feel it difficult to get people to leave, ask the midwife to do it for you.

If you've had your baby at home, or once your partner and baby return from the hospital, it is even more important to regulate the number of visitors. If nothing else, it's vital that you don't use up all of your paternity leave on managing a parade of family and friends. Encourage friends to phone first and don't be afraid of putting them off for a day or two. You may like seeing a few people every day, or prefer visitors on alternate days – just don't allow yourselves to become overwhelmed. Remember that real friends won't mind being asked not to come round for a while. Don't plan too far ahead; instead, see how you feel from day to day.

Encourage people who have been unwell, with infectious illnesses, however minor, to delay visiting until they are fully recovered.

Cake, please!

If you can, get your visitors to work for you, not the other way round. If you need something from the shops, why not ask them to pick it up on their way over? Alternatively, ask them to bring a cake or similar with them and get them to be 'refreshments monitor' when they arrive, or help you doing something practical while your partner rests. The liberating realization you'll probably have is that people love being asked to help, because they enjoy the sense of feeling needed.

Managing the grandparents

For many mums and dads of new parents, becoming 'Granny' or 'Grandad' is a fantastic privilege and as much a life-changer for them as it is for you. A bit of self-indulgence on their part is perfectly reasonable and they can become a key source of support as you navigate first-time parenthood. However, for some, grandparents also create a tricky paradox. You'll have a new appreciation for their role as parents and the challenges they themselves faced. However you'll probably also have the feeling that you need to assert yourselves as new parents, without outside interference. You're the ones who are responsible for raising this child and you've got to be able to do it on your own. You may want to ask for a grandparent's advice on certain issues (there's nothing like a new baby to bring forward loads of advice from everyone), but don't feel that you have to take it.

Now and then you may encounter a parenting culture-clash between you and your own parents (or in-laws). Before worrying about them, check that you and your partner are agreed on the best way to broach any potentially inflammatory issues. Once you're agreed, bite the bullet! If your parents do something you do not approve of, summon up all your sensitivity and tell them. If you don't do it at the beginning, it will only get harder to do later on. The real key to success with family and friends is to keep them involved; it will help them and help you. But be clear that asking for advice is not an open invitation to interfere.

Condensed idea
Invite people to join in the celebrations but don't overstretch yourselves

(32) More than one

Around the world, the number of multiple births is growing. Whether they were conceived naturally or through fertility treatment, they bring their own, very specific challenges. Not least because twins or triplets (or more) often demand attention at the same time.

You're a superdad now!

Friends of mine recently had twins and I can see still picture the dad's face when he first told me the news. His eyes told a story of sheer delight, mixed with a substantial undercurrent of shock, disbelief and mild panic. The babies weren't even born yet, but he walked around in a daze for weeks. He's since taken to the realities of multiple fatherhood like the proverbial duck to water and he's loving every minute of it. Well, almost. Though I guarantee he can't sit through the first two minutes of a TV show without dropping off.

Of course, all the principles for being a 'singleton' parent still apply, but the learning curve gets steeper the more kids you add. The problem is, 'steeper' doesn't really cover it. Try 'exponential' instead. The main challenge is one of pure logistics – from the moment your babies are born, you will embark on a relentless search for easier ways to get things done. Many simple things may seem impossible at first but, over time, you'll discover your own inner multi-tasker. You'll find yourself doing great feats of baby handling and childcare that will leave other dads gasping in awe and wonderment.

> Lovely twins. Too tired to tweet.
> #dadtotwoatonce

How common are twins and other multiple pregnancies?

The incidence of twins, triplets and (deep breath) higher multiple pregnancies are on the increase. More and more women are benefitting from the technological advances in assisted conception, but these treatments greatly increase a woman's chance of having more than one baby at the same time. The odds of having multiples are influenced by many factors, but large studies in the USA suggest that assisted conception there has led to a twin birth occurring once in every 32 births. For women who conceive without medical intervention a twin birth occurs once in every 80–90 cases (rates vary from country to country).

The early 1980s saw a huge rise in the incidence of triplets and quadruplets as the use of fertility treatments became more commonplace. However, recent years have seen these techniques become more sophisticated and the incidence of higher-order multiple births has come down to reflect this.

In the early days, don't worry that feeding and caring for the babies dominates your day. As your confidence in understanding and responding to your babies' needs begins to grow, things will become quicker and easier. Only parents who have experienced the twins or triplets phenomenon for themselves can truly understand what's involved, so make the most of their support and know-how. Ask your midwife for details of the local twins and multiple birth support group. The clearest advice from 'been there' parents seems to be not to bear the additional workload on your own. Get help. Ask visitors to take care of you as well as the babies. The Internet is awash with discussion forums for mums and dads of multiple babies, and these can be hugely useful sources of information, support and encouragement as you find your feet. If you can, get online yourself and connect with other people in a similar situation to you.

Feeding lots of babies

Some mums very successfully breastfeed more than one baby. Triangular pillows are widely available and a good investment for any new mum, but even more so if she's feeding two at once. She can put the pillow on her lap so that it supports both children and this makes it much easier to feed them at the same time. If you are bottle-feeding twins (or more), consider buying different coloured bottle tops, and always use the same colour for each baby. The big plus here is that when you are feeding the babies simultaneously, and stop feeding them to wind one, you will not get confused as to which bottle is whose.

Buying for two

It's tempting, but don't overdo the equipment. Two or three times as many babies needn't mean two or three times as much stuff. In all likelihood, you'll be amazed at the amount of stuff you'll be given as soon as they're born. Everybody loves a new baby, but twins or triplets really do seem to be a licence for others to splash out. Talk to experienced parents about what the essentials are and stick to them at first.

There's one thing to beware: if you have same sex twins or triplets, you will be given sets of identical outfits unless you put the word out early on that you'd prefer to dress them differently.

Out and about

Make the most of Internet shopping to take the stress out of the big 'weekly food shop' supermarket trips. You can then concentrate on less challenging – and therefore more enjoyable – trips out to pick up smaller items. If you don't have access to the Internet, consider asking a friend or family member to shop for you online from time to time.

After a while, you may find that although negotiating a shopping trip is hardly the ideal recipe for a stress-free day, you're keen to face the challenge as part of getting back to 'normal'. Check out your local shops to see which are twin- or triplet-friendly (a common complaint amongst parents is that many are not). See, for example, how many supermarket trolleys are suitable for more than one small baby and politely let Customer Services know if there aren't enough. You're a superdad now and this is your chance to make things better for dads after you.

New parents of twins or triplets often put off going out alone with their babies for some time after the birth; it can seem like a worrying prospect. But as with so much in parenthood, the advice from most parents who have been there themselves is 'just jump in and do it'. Chances are that it won't be as bad as you think and every time you go out, you'll get better and quicker at doing it (be prepared for very slow outings in the early days). The biggest hurdle you'll face is achieving anything at all when everyone just wants to stop you and admire your babies.

Condensed idea
Being a father of twins or more propels you into the rank of Superdad

(33) Remember sleep?

Sleep, or rather the lack of it, features largely in the first few months weeks of parenthood. Most small babies seem almost nocturnal: sound asleep during the day, unbelievably perky at night. There are no quick fixes – it's just a case of feeling your way, one day at a time.

Eyes wide open

Sleep deprivation is one of the earliest known forms of torture and becoming the parent of a newborn baby girl or boy gives every mum and dad the chance to have an impromptu, living history lesson. Broken nights are the last thing you need while simultaneously recovering from the birth, grappling with your new roles and keeping the rest of your life in balance, but it's an unavoidable rite of passage. The trick is to work smarter, not just harder.

> An alarm clock is something people without kids use to wake up. #upalready

Next door's baby sleeps all day...

Most newborns drift in and out of sleep during the day and night, feeding little and often. Pregnancy or labour complications and premature birth can influence early sleeping patterns. For example, babies who have had a forceps or ventouse delivery will sometimes sleep little, be very restless and cry a lot, mainly due to the monumental headache they have as they recover from the birth.

Around the age of six weeks or so, babies tend to wake up more. They need feeding roughly every two to four hours, but can sleep between feeds for twenty minutes or a couple of hours. Every baby needs a different amount of sleep and yours will have his own way of doing things too. If you ask around you'll discover that there is a wide range of 'normal' and your baby's sleeping habits probably fit well within it. As the weeks go by your baby will spend more time awake between feeds

and will gradually become more interested in the world around him. He may wake earlier but not be ready for a feed. Instead, he may want some stimulation – looking at your face, watching tree branches moving in the wind, or looking at mobiles against the light.

Get with the programme

There's been a lot written about the importance of sleep routines over the years, but these don't really apply to babies less than three months old. So before he gets to that age, you can have fun experimenting with different ways of getting him off to sleep. There are no hard and fast rules: ask other parents and prepare to be amazed at the variety of solutions they've found, from soothing music and dim lights to rock music and twinkling nightlights. Every baby is different and you'll soon discover what suits you and your child. As you're pondering how to help him sleep, you might want to start thinking about a routine that will suit you and your partner as your baby gets older. At three to four months old, your baby's habits – both good and bad – will start to become more fixed, so creating some boundaries and structure from around two months on will help him to sleep well in the long run.

Safe sleeping

It's not known why some (thankfully very few) babies die suddenly and for no apparent reason, but it must be one of a new parent's greatest fears. Huge research programmes have meant that the incidence of Sudden Infant Death Syndrome (SIDS or 'cot death') has dramatically reduced over the past few years, so don't let worry about this stop you from enjoying your baby's first few months. However, it's good to know that you can reduce the risk for your baby by following the advice given below.

- Place your baby on his back to sleep, in a cot in the same room as you.
- Don't smoke during pregnancy or let anyone smoke in the same room as your baby.
- Don't share a bed with your baby if you've been drinking alcohol, if you take drugs or if you're a smoker.
- Never sleep with your baby on a sofa or armchair.
- Don't let your baby get too hot.
- Keep your baby's head uncovered. His blanket should be tucked in no higher than his shoulders.
- Place your baby in the 'feet to foot' position (with his feet at the end of the cot or pram).

Sleep basics

Following a few general rules early on can help your baby, your partner and you to crack the sleep habit. First of all, your baby needs to distinguish night from day. You can help him by adopting the tried-and-tested 'I'm so dull to be with at night but a top entertainer in the day' approach. Don't play with him at night; be responsive and meet his needs, but don't waken him more than he already is. Nature will help you in this to a certain extent – when you're exhausted, your usual happy-go-lucky self may go off on a short sabbatical anyway. Once his bedtime has arrived, feed and change him during the night in subdued lighting and maintain a quiet, bland atmosphere.

Second, share the task with your partner, but plan it out carefully and together. If she is breastfeeding, there is no getting away from the fact that she will be up more than you in the night. If you are working, you'll need to work out how to get some sleep at night in order to function. At weekends, however (or days off), consider doing a couple of night shifts with your baby. Even with a breastfeeding baby, a bit of organization means you can give him previously expressed and stored breast milk and feeding him yourself can be a really special experience. The added bonus will be the amazing difference a regular night (or two) of uninterrupted sleep can make for your partner's wellbeing. Alternatively, strike a deal between yourselves: one of you doing the early shift every night (attending to the baby between, say bedtime and 3 a.m.), while the other does the second shift (3 a.m. until 8 a.m.). However you cope, the important thing is to talk about it with each other. That way you'll avoid either of feeling resentful that the other isn't pulling their weight. At weekends you can give each other a bit of time off, during the day and night.

Third, try getting other people involved. If grandparents, aunts and uncles volunteer to have baby overnight – even just once – and you can cope with leaving him, take them up on the offer. Be sure to give yourself a break; don't try to play the superhero. Although you might normally avoid sleeping during the day, this is a good time to practise a new habit if possible. A rested dad is probably a better dad.

Condensed idea
Sleep deprivation comes with the territory but you can get through it

Cry baby

Many first-time parents are surprised by quite how much babies cry. During the first weeks, learning to interpret what your baby is saying can be like learning a new language with someone yelling in your ear. This phase will pass, but it can be stressful.

How loud?

When babies cry, they make a lot of noise. In fact, the average baby's cry measures around 110 decibels. For comparison, this the same as a car horn and only 10 decibels less than an emergency siren or thunder. That sounds almost unbelievable, until you hear a baby really get her motor running for a crying session and start to wonder if perhaps the

anonymous measurer got those levels the wrong way round. Within the confines of a small room, even a small baby's lung capacity is pretty impressive.

Before she develops other means to tell you what she wants or how she feels, crying is your baby's only method of communication. Be prepared; some babies are more vocal than others. Others may cry, at varying volume, for no apparent reason. Studies looking at newborn babies in the 1960s found that, on average, they cried for 1.75 hours per day during the second week of life, increasing to

> Whoever invented earplugs should have been awarded the Nobel Peace Prize #apologiestotheneighbours

2.75 at six weeks. Further research in the USA has since confirmed these findings – it suggests that crying reaches a peak of three hours a day by six weeks. Fortunately, babies don't usually put in their daily two-hour crying stint all at once (though on occasions it might feel like they do) and the amount of crying will normally subside by three months, remaining constant from that point until they are about a year old. Contrary to popular belief, research also indicates that first babies do not tend to cry more than subsequent children. Nor do breastfed babies cry any more than bottle-fed babies, so if yours is breastfed and cries a lot, changing to bottle-feeding is unlikely to result in her crying less.

There are several distinctly different ways of crying. Some babies start with a whimper and gradually build to a crescendo, while others accelerate immediately to 110 decibels and just stay there. As time goes by, you and your partner will quickly learn to recognize your own child's cry and get to know what different cries mean. Ask yourself whether she has some kind of physical need. For instance, does she need feeding or changing? Is she too hot or cold? Check that she's not uncomfortable, either in her position or clothes. Is she in pain? Signals might include drawing up her knees or vomiting. She may be tired but wired – babies

Tips for soothing a crying baby

If your baby is crying, always talk to her in a calm, soft, quiet, way (no matter how irritated or anxious you feel yourself). And remember that some babies just feel like having a cry for no real reason.

- Pick her up and cuddle her – let her hear your heartbeat.
- Place a warm hand on her stomach or chest.
- Lay your baby tummy down across your lap (her head supported) and rub her back, or sway your knees from side to side.
- Rock her in your arms, or take her for a walk in a buggy or a baby sling.
- Distract your baby with an interesting sight such as fish swimming in a tank or a torch shining on a wall.
- Turn on some quiet music and slow dance together.
- Letting her suck on something – her fist or a clean finger.
- If it's a warm room, take her clothes off – some babies love it.
- Give her a warm bath.
- Put her in her car seat and take her for a drive.
- Put her near household noises – the background hum of a vacuum cleaner or fan is similar to sounds she was used to in the womb.

often find it hard to switch off, particularly if they are over-tired or have been over-stimulated. Or she may just want to be held: small babies need lots of physical comfort in the early months. Confusingly, babies can also cry for no real reason. As the months pass, your baby will learn other ways of communicating with you, through eye contact, noises and smiling, all of which will reduce her need to cry for attention.

Learning to distinguish one cry from another is a bit of an art, but you'll be surprised how quickly you'll pick it up. For instance, some babies will wait while you change them prior to a feed, but others want to be fed NOW! As a general rule, distressed babies respond better to being handled confidently, so work through the possibilities as though you know exactly what you're doing, even as you're trying to work it out.

Be Kind to yourselves

Mums in particular can find a crying baby a stressful experience. If your newborn seems to cry almost constantly, he won't do himself lasting harm but it's likely to be hard going. Your partner may tend to blame herself when actually it has very little to do with anything either of you are doing. Sometimes simply accepting that you have a baby who cries a lot – while coping as well as you can – may be the first step in getting through this difficult phase.

If you've met your baby's immediate needs and tried everything you can to calm her but nothing has worked, look after each other instead. Try to stay calm. If you or your partner are upset, anxious or feeling like you can't cope, it is okay to put your baby in her cot and to let her cry for short spells (15 minutes or so) out of your range of hearing. If you can, find a place to which you can retreat to relax – even for a moment or two. Take deep breaths and, if it helps calm you, put on some quiet music. If you're beginning to climb the walls and you've tried everything, call a friend or relative for support. Give yourself a break and let someone else take over for a while. It's also a good idea to ask your midwife or another health professional about coping strategies.

Condensed idea
As your baby grows, he'll find new ways of communicating with you and the crying will stop

(35) Bragging

When you become a dad and your partner becomes a mum, you'll get to know many other couples with children of a similar age. This is a supportive environment, but keep an eye out for the competitive parent. Most of all, resist the urge to become one yourself.

Keeping up with the Joneses

As you approach the end of your first few weeks as a dad, you may find yourself feeling fairly satisfied about how things are turning out. Why, you're almost a veteran. While it will still feel like the broken nights are never-ending, you'll be amazed at how much has happened and astonished at how quickly time has flown since your baby son or daughter was born. You're probably more confident about your role as a dad and finding that you're doing things more instinctively than before. You'll also have a few great tricks, that you've either worked out for yourself or been given by other people. Overall, things are getting easier.

> All the other babies seem to be crawling already. Wish James would hurry up! #pushyparent

You and your partner will probably also be getting out and about a bit more, beginning to mix with other people, whether this is at clinics, at antenatal group 'meet ups' or back at work. In particular, you'll probably find yourself spending a fair amount of time with parents of children around the same age as your own. After the strange cocooning feeling around the birth period, it will feel great to start socializing again, albeit a very different life from the one you were living pre-baby. Spending time with other parents is important, because it's great to share your successes (and sometimes spectacular failures) with others going through the same thing. But it does raise an interesting social phenomenon: that of the competitive parent.

'Two weeks old and already reading'

Who knows what fires the competitive urge in a new mum or dad? Deep down we all like to win, but new parents can really take the proverbial biscuit. Is he sleeping the best? Is he feeding the best? Is he smiling first? Has he got his first tooth? Is he sitting up? Has he passed his driving test? The list goes on and on, with proud (but often insecure) parents scoring points off one another in an attempt to claim the imaginary title of

Real developmental worries

While it's certainly important to keep a bit of perspective once you hit the new parent social circuit, don't completely blank out developmental stages. In the early weeks of your baby's life he will receive a number of health checks to make sure that he's growing well and also to highlight whether there are any potential problems to keep an eye on. If you have a genuine worry about your child's health, development, or general wellbeing, never hesitate to call your midwife or doctor. All healthcare professionals have a golden rule: trust a parent's instinct. Great importance is placed upon a mum and dad's ability to sense when something just isn't right and they will always listen to you, taking any concerns over young babies very seriously. If in doubt, make the call – you'll never be sorry that you did.

'most advanced child'. This is all very well as long as you can take it with a pinch of salt. The problem is that when you want the best for your son, but you're exhausted from lack of sleep and still learning the ropes of parenthood, it's really easy to lose perspective. Sometimes the way things are worded 'Oh, so your baby isn't doing that yet then?' can cut right to the heart of the questions spinning around in your own head, 'Is he OK?' and 'Am I doing OK for him?' In the early months, with their day almost entirely centred around looking after the baby, new mums can feel it particularly acutely.

There's no perfect time

The fact is that all babies develop at different rates. Some sit up and crawl early on, some don't; some sleep well from day one, and others don't. Get used to it. Focus instead on enjoying being a fantastic father and telling your partner that she is a marvellous mum. The penny dropped for me when I was talking with a friend about how, some way into early parenthood, we were a little concerned that Jack wasn't walking yet. Well-meaning comments from loving grandparents had added to our anxiety. My friend simply pointed out that he had never walked down the street, thinking to himself of each passerby, 'they must have been an early walker'. Strangely, neither had I. No one ever admires an adult's 'expressive gait' and concludes that he must have been further down the developmental trail than his mates at nursery. Underneath the race to be the first, we all know deep down that it's not when they do it that's important, it's whether they do it. Looking back we're a little sheepish about the things that once made us anxious. Despite the 'late start', Jack now walks with the best of them. In fact, having become a strapping teenager, it's now we've really got things to worry about!

Every dad wants the best for his baby, as does every mum, but do your best to rise above the occasional competitive parent comment and resist the urge to join in yourself. That way madness lies. Try not to become too preoccupied with what he can and can't do. Your child will develop at a speed that suits him and, frankly, there's little you can do about it. Some

things he'll learn quickly; others will take him longer to get the hang of. Just keep in mind that it's all perfectly normal and that's the way humans are meant to be.

My guess is that the first hot topic will be sleep. Do your best to avoid comparing your own baby's sleeping pattern with the experiences of other parents – you'll either be disheartened or end up feeling so smug that you lose all your friends who are finding things tough. Remember, that there's no such thing as the perfect parent or perfect baby. It's easy to project to the outside world an image that is carefully crafted with the rougher edges smoothed off. But the truth is that the people who freely tell everyone what a breeze parenthood is and how marvellously they're coping, may not be representing the reality of what is happening behind closed doors. Just relax, say nothing and smile.

Condensed idea
Beware competitive parents and resist the urge to become one yourself

36 Sex after the birth

It's entirely possible for your love life to return to something like normality after the arrival of your baby. But you do need to give it time. Listen to your partner – she will probably be feeling battered and bruised for some time, so be understanding and be patient.

When can we have sex?

There's an old joke about a guy picking up a book called 'Sex after Children', which turns out to have 250 blank pages (boom cha!). However, while there's no doubt that, after children, you and your partner's sex life will change, if lovemaking has been a healthy part of your relationship before the baby, there's no reason why it shouldn't be again. The main thing is to work it out together.

Many mums (more than you may think) report that their partners think they'll be ready for sex as soon as they get home from hospital. So if you were thinking that yourself, do your partner a favour and think about what she's just been through, bearing in mind that she's just given birth and may have stitches in all the most awkward places. Give her all the time she needs to recover physically from the birth, adjust to the demands of new motherhood and get used to the idea of intimacy again. Take your lead from her.

Some couples wait just a few weeks, others months, others longer still. Health professionals have traditionally counselled against couples engaging in penetrative sex until after the woman has been given the go-ahead at her six-week, postnatal check-up. You could, however, try making love just before the check-up so that you can discuss any issues with the doctor.

Stay connected

New parents experience a rollercoaster of emotions – highs can be followed by anxiety and even depression. Childbirth involves huge hormonal and emotional changes, alongside the physical challenges, so be sensitive to your partner. Whilst some mums find they recover from the birth quickly, many still feel unsexy for a time and simply don't feel like sex.

It's also not unusual for a dad to find the delivery quite a traumatic experience and consequently feel the same way. Exhaustion can mean a lowering, even absence, of sex drive for either of you.

Give yourself time. Don't rush into things until you're both ready. Be sensitive to one another's feelings. As any relationship expert will tell you, the best lovemaking is founded on a basis of mutual trust, love and respect. Even in the maelstrom of early parenthood, do your best to keep communication open and try to understand each other's point of view. Once you feel ready, begin gently. Choose a time in the day when you're less likely to be exhausted and disturbed by the baby (or anyone else). When you finally decide to opt for full sex, it's a good idea to choose a position in which your partner can control the pace and depth of penetration. Vaginal dryness can be a problem and, if so, use a lubricating cream or gel. Even if she's breastfeeding, and as long as they're not too tender, caressing your partner's breasts is fine, but be prepared for the occasional jet of milk! Practically speaking, if the baby has had a feed a little while beforehand, this is less likely to happen. Overall, be patient with each other and you'll soon find yourselves getting back into the swing of things.

Stay protected

Before you resume your sex life, think about contraception. Your midwife or doctor will ask your partner about this soon after the delivery. The risks of falling pregnant again soon after giving birth are quite high. If you are lucky enough to be getting some action relatively soon after the baby

How to turn up the heat

You might find you have to seduce your partner all over again, as though you've just met. So don't underestimate the power of setting the mood. Go the extra mile – romantic gestures, relaxing baths, gentle massages and mood lighting will all help your partner feel like a 'normal woman' again.

- Your partner may not feel great about her body after childbirth. Telling her how much you love her body will help her feel better about herself.
- Help her to know that you love her as a woman, not just as the mother of your child.
- If you are struggling to control your sex drive, talk to your male friends or doctor about it. Evidence shows that new dads are vulnerable to affairs, which are, in themselves, destructive – so do your best to make sure it doesn't happen to you.
- Take advantage of offers of babysitting from friends and family. Going out together will help you reconnect as a couple.
- Share the parenting workload. Remind yourself that the men who have the best sex lives are probably the ones whose partners get the most sleep.

is born, remember that, whatever Tommy Macfarlane told you in the playground at school, breastfeeding is not a reliable form of contraception. Furthermore a woman's periods can vary considerably following delivery so, until your partner has re-established her cycle, natural methods of family planning may not be a reliable way of avoiding pregnancy. The contraception options open to you as a couple will vary according to whether your partner is breastfeeding or not and whether she had any complications during her pregnancy. As a couple, you may not favour condoms for long-term use, but they are very useful if you want to wait a while before deciding on a more permanent method of contraception.

Stay creative

Even if full sex isn't immediately on the horizon, don't disregard all the other ways to be intimate with one another. Being physically close and cuddling, without penetration, can rekindle the connection between you and your partner and help keep your relationship healthy. Exploring each other's bodies, perhaps mutual masturbation if you want, can be a way of

> Our post-baby sex life? Mind your own business! #atweet2far

giving each other pleasure and finding out what is comfortable for both of you. Try to view the sex issue not so much as a wall to be scaled, but more an opportunity to think a little laterally. When you have a baby, the terms of reference change: from sex whenever you want, to sex in 'stolen moments'. Over time, many couples find that this spices up their sex life more than they could have imagined.

Condensed idea
Getting back into sex may take some time, but keep talking and it will be worth the wait

At times, getting the balance right between your myriad responsibilities as a dad, partner, employee and so on, can make scaling the north face of the Eiger seem like a picnic in the park. But finding ways to keep yourself healthy – physically, emotionally and socially – is vital.

Cabin pressure

If you have ever travelled on a plane, you'll know that just before take-off one of the cabin staff makes the obligatory announcements about what to do in case of an emergency. Have you ever noticed, however, that mums and dads get a little extra advice? 'For parents of young children, please ensure you fasten your own oxygen mask before attempting to secure someone else's.' At first, this seems counter-intuitive; wouldn't your priority be to save your daughter before attempting to save yourself? The airlines however, have realized something that we don't immediately appreciate. If you are struggling for breath yourself, you are less likely to be able to fasten an oxygen mask over the head of your frightened, panicky child. This follows through for all situations in life; if you don't look after yourself and make sure you are physically and mentally fit, you won't be of much use to anyone else.

The first few months of parenthood are the most wonderful but in some ways, the toughest. Life as a dad is always going to be full of surprises but early fatherhood really does feel like being thrown in at the deep end. It's all about finding your feet and coping. Some new parents spend virtually every waking moment either working or caring for their child, and forget to create a little 'oasis' of time for themselves. As a result, they're almost permanently exhausted, and never really feel on top of things. The mistake they make is that, though they may feel that they're coping, they're really not. So amidst the feeding, rocking, changing, bathing, playing and visitor coordinating, make sure you pay attention to your own needs too.

Check your oxygen levels

'Sanity time' is a vital part of any parent's day. No matter what you do to get it, try to establish good habits early on. It might be a walk in the fresh air, or an undisturbed read of the paper on a Saturday morning; it might be knocking up a culinary masterpiece or knocking seven bells out of a punch bag at the gym. Do whatever works for you.

Finding a balance

If you've ever watched a tightrope walker, you'll be able to picture him and the sense of poise he displays as he steps out on to the wire. From a distance, he seems rock steady, but successful tightrope walking actually depends on a steady head guiding continual, small adjustments to keep the artist upright and on the rope.

As a dad, finding time for yourself is vital, but it's important to keep an eye on your own balance too. Your new-found enthusiasm for cycling, ceramics or scuba diving in the name of sanity isn't a licence to abdicate your responsibilities as a father – it's about helping you to be a better dad, a better partner, a better person. As your daughter grows, and as circumstances change, keep your head steady. Learn to look at yourself and make continual adjustments to the priorities in your life. It will help her, and you, strike the healthy balance you both need.

It may take a little organization and perhaps a little give and take with your partner about how long and how often each of you does what, but work as a team to sort something out. You may be surprised how little time you actually need to feel refreshed and ready to face the world again. Recognize that you need to help your partner find sanity time too, which can be tricky, as some new mums need considerable convincing that the baby can do without them, even for a little while.

Keep in shape and eat well

I know it's not very interesting (and who can resist the lure of the late night curry?), but you will feel better, both physically and emotionally, if you exercise and eat well. There's a lot to do in fatherhood – running around parks, teaching her to swim, ride a bike, and much more – so, although your washboard stomach may forever have a little more laundry on it than you would ideally like, it still makes sense to keep yourself fit and healthy as you're going to need a body that is built for action.

Cut out eating between meals and watch your alcohol intake. Kebabs needn't be entirely off the menu, but make sure you balance your diet with plenty of fruit and fresh vegetables. Find a form of exercise that you enjoy, ideally with friends who will toughen your resolve to stick at it.

Time for two

With divorce and separation statistics continuing to rise, it's clear that sustaining a long-term relationship isn't easy. Every couple needs the chance to nurture their relationship: spending time together, communicating and sharing their lives. As you think about your average week, make this a priority for you. Enjoy being parents

> Fantastic – a night out at last! Not a nappy, wet wipe or buggy in sight. (I wonder how the baby's doing...) #boysnightout

together. Even when you don't feel like it, quit your TV-dinner habit, making time for conversation which is based on more than 'Where's the remote control?'. Ask your partner about the day she's had. Avoid letting sex become a major issue (see pages 24–27).

Keep in touch with friends

In the hurly burly of fatherhood, make sure you don't allow the contact you have with your wider circle of family and friends to lapse. You'll need to draw on the support and strength that these relationships provide as you navigate the months and years ahead. You'll need people to laugh with you (sometimes at you), listen to you and cry with you too. They'll need you to do the same for them. Get your diary out and book in time, even if it seems a long way off. It will leave you better equipped to be the dad, and the person, that you, your partner and your child want you to be.

Condensed idea
While fulfilling your role as 'action dad', make sure you look after yourself too

38 Baby blues

Having felt euphoric immediately after delivery, many new mums feel tearful around three days later. These 'baby blues' normally subside quickly, but some women experience more serious postnatal depression and it's important that you are alert to the symptoms.

Getting the blues

Baby blues are different to depression. They are so common that they are pretty much regarded as normal for a new mum. They are short term (from just a few days to a few weeks) and manageable. However, they're still not much fun for your partner, with symptoms including sleeplessness (even when she gets the chance), loss of appetite, sadness and anxiety that she's not up to the job of being a mum.

What is postnatal depression?

Postnatal depression (PND) affects about one in 10 women. It can surface for a mum at any time within the first year following the birth of a child, but it is most common amongst mothers of babies who are between four and six months old. PND affects different women in different ways but is characterized by feeling irritable, tired and tearful, and strangely distanced from their baby. Women with postnatal depression also complain of an inability to concentrate, feeling confused and inadequate, both in terms of caring for their baby and in other relationships. Mums can be reluctant to talk to health professionals

> I love you Jenny and so proud of you. You looked beautiful today. Loving being dad with you as mum. #proudpartner

about their depression because they are worried that it will 'expose' them as 'bad mothers', and lead to their baby being taken away from them.

There are many reasons why women suffer from PND. It can vary in its severity but also in the way it strikes, appearing gradually or suddenly without much warning. There is evidence that women are more prone to postnatal depression if they have just given birth to their first child, have a history of suffering from premenstrual depression, or were depressed during their pregnancy. Some doctors suggest that it's all down to changes in hormone levels, others that it's related to the huge adjustments, both mentally and physically that a woman goes through post-birth. The main thing is to keep a look out for the signs and be supportive of your partner, encouraging her to seek help, if necessary.

The signs of PND

In addition to the general symptoms given above, women can experience feelings of despondency, hopelessness and lethargy, taking little interest in anything or anyone. They can feel guilty that they do not love their

Postnatal depression in men

PND doesn't just affect mums. In recent years, it has been increasingly recognized that dads can be affected too, as they come to terms with the responsibilities of fatherhood, changing relationships and lifestyle, financial pressures and a greater workload at home. Some suggest that as many as one in 25 dads may be affected. If you feel yourself becoming depressed:

- Don't ignore it. It is *not* better to soldier on by yourself.
- Don't wait to be asked – actively seek out assistance from the health professionals.
- Avoid retreating into alcohol, drugs or other potentially destructive activities. In the long run it will do more harm than good.
- Don't become a workaholic – this has the potential to damage your relationship with your partner and baby and won't do anything to sort out the issues.
- Remember that your health is important to you, your baby and your partner. They want and need you to be in good shape.
- Remember, the sooner you recognize the problem, the sooner you can sort it out.

baby enough but, paradoxically also obsess about his health and general wellbeing. Some mums experience panic attacks or overwhelming anxiety about minor things that wouldn't normally bother them at all. Women with PND often lose all interest in sex and become indifferent, occasionally even hostile, to their partners. Sometimes, PND manifests itself in a physical way, through head and stomach aches or blurred vision. Postnatal depression is a serious condition, but there are ways through.

Ways to help

The early symptoms of depression are usually first noticed by partners and wider family and friends, rather than by the mum herself. In fact, it is not uncommon for the sufferer to vehemently deny that there is a problem. This is completely understandable, because your partner is likely to be very frightened by the emotions she feels. The important thing to remember is that no one is immune to this condition; depression can hit anyone. It will be your job to help your partner to realize that it is no reflection upon her as a person or on her ability as a mother.

If you suspect that your partner may be suffering from postnatal depression, talk to your midwife or doctor as soon as possible. The symptoms may diminish after a few weeks, but there are lots of general things you can do to support your partner in the meantime. Give her the chance to talk to you, while you listen sensitively, without judging her. Encourage her (making arrangements if necessary) to spend time with her friends and family, but also provide her as often as you can with opportunities to relax and rest. Help your partner to look after herself – gently make sure she gets dressed in the morning, buy her nutritious snacks, cook her a healthy meal, or encourage her to do some gentle physical activity with you or with friends. These little differences can change things for the better and help your partner begin to cope again. PND usually gets better in time, but your patience will be tested while it does, so don't let impatience get the better of you. If symptoms persist, make sure you get help, rather than struggling on alone. Correct medication and/or counselling can help your partner recover. Remember – it's a common problem, there is help available and there's no reason why either of you should suffer alone.

Condensed idea
Postnatal depression is tough, but you can both get through it

(39) Networking

Building and engaging with a supportive network of friends and family will help you though the good times and the bad times ahead. Find trusted friends to whom you can talk to about the joys, needs, aspirations and difficulties of being a first time dad.

Easier with others

Have you ever wondered why friends who are having babies seem to meet people at antenatal groups and then continue to see them long after their babies have been born? Have you considered, too, why it is that dads who, pre-kids, would have run a mile from a group of small children, suddenly feel drawn to go on holiday with other families who have lots of young kids themselves? There's the 'we're all the same stage of life' reason of course, but many mums and dads would also admit that it's just easier with other people around. As soon as dads come skidding into fatherhood, and mums into motherhood, we come up against the indisputable realization that, however superhuman we thought we were before we entered it, we can't do this parenting business successfully on our own. We need a support system.

You know it makes sense

The fact is we all need support networks of some form or other. We need them ourselves to thrive generally, and we need them once we have kids to help us give them a balanced upbringing. Above all, networks are practical. The people in our new-parent network will give us advice on all sorts of things, from suggesting ways to help stop a baby crying to the best places to go on a rainy day. They're likely to have secondhand gear and clothing that could save us a fortune, and know the number of a babysitter who can be called upon at short notice. Over the years, you'll find that these are the people you're likely to call upon to pick up your child from school when you find yourself stuck in a traffic jam, or share lifts with to far-flung children's parties. These friends are a vital support network for people who don't have family living around them, and indispensible whatever your situation. A good network will provide entertainment and advice, and save you time, money and heartache (there are few more stressful things than being late to pick up a child

How to build a network

Dads who are in similar situations to you can prove to be a goldmine of information, giving you plenty of reassurance and practical help. They can provide advice on the things you're struggling with (whether these are practical or emotional) and share their triumphs and mistakes. Here's a few ideas for ways to find a network near you:

- Ask your doctor, midwife or health visitor about any local 'new-dads' groups.
- Check all the local 'community hubs', such as the library, leisure centre and health centre, for information about new-dads groups.
- Do go online, but use it to check out your offline options.
- Faith groups offer fantastic supportive communities. Check out your local church, synagogue or mosque and see what's going on.
- Recognize that a support network is more than one-way traffic. Your honesty, experiences, insights and ideas will help other dads every little bit as much as theirs will help you.

and having no one else to call upon). As a bloke, you'll also get one other really valuable thing from the new-dad network: an outlet to talk about the things that really matter to you. Of course, your partner will always be a first port of call, but there are some things you might not want to discuss with her, for all sorts of reasons. We get a sense of what's 'normal' in any situation by checking out what our peers are up to, and we might only be able to discuss our fears with another bloke who we know has faced a similar situation. Parenthood is uncharted territory, and a network of dads (and mums!) can help keep us on the straight and narrow.

> A friend is someone who knows all about you and still likes you.
> #goodmates

Doing it for the Kids

And of course networks aren't just about helping you do your parenting job better; they're also about helping your child grow into a rounded, balanced person. The often-quoted proverb, 'It takes a village to raise a child' sums it up beautifully. Raising kids is a communal effort that goes way beyond the biological family; friends, neighbours, teachers, spiritual leaders, sports coaches, and all sorts of people will play a role. There's a balance to be struck of course – it's not a licence for interference and opinion from all and sundry; and quality, not quantity is the name of the game.

Get real

Building networks, however, isn't always easy. Many of us live far more individual, autonomous lives, than even relatively recent generations. Men in particular, tend to work long hours, with little spare time. Many of us come from families that are geographically dispersed and it's easy to end up paying more attention to our virtual social networks than

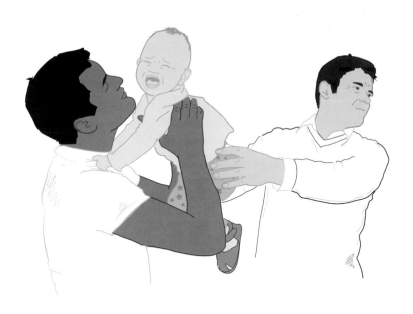

our physical ones. While virtual communities have their place, they can't beat real life. It's perhaps ironic that our online profiles might be beautifully crafted but we still don't know the names of the people who live down the street. Sometimes we all need to be reminded of the value of real family relationships, real shared responsibility, authentic generosity and genuine interdependence.

Think of ways you can receive support yourself while also helping other parents too. It may take a bit of organizing and more than a little courage to make the move but check out what's going on locally for you. Groups for new dads and new mums are springing up all the time. Check the box on page 157 for ideas, then pick up the phone and join in.

Condensed idea
Building a physical, not virtual, network of dads will keep you grounded

40 Work-life balance

Every dad who has had to learn to balance work life with home life will readily identify the tensions that come with trying to accommodate the insistent demands of both. Maintaining a healthy balance is tough but achievable.

Decide what's important to you

For new dads, returning to work after the birth of a baby can be a shock to the system. Sometimes it's literally a wake-up call. After all, when you become a dad, you're taking on a second job, and one that didn't come with any induction training from the HR department. Simple things can quickly become maddeningly difficult to achieve. When you have been up half the night or were about to go to work but found yourself called upon to soothe a crying baby, even getting to work on time can seem like a major achievement.

The pressure from being pulled in two or more directions at once, as the conflicting expectations of new family and existing job collide, can be stressful and exhausting. But be encouraged: the fact that you feel the pressure of being a working parent is a sign that you want to be the best dad you can be as well as a responsible worker. It's normal, natural and even healthy to feel the tension of your competing responsibilities.

Consider your options

Assuming that at least one person in the family has to work to enable you to live, kids and work are part of the complex juggling act of life in the 21st century. In the UK, 66 per cent of mothers are in employment,

Ways to strike a balance

Becoming a dad will change the way you think about work. It's both more important than ever (financially) while perhaps also less important to you than before (because your baby has taken centre stage). The following tips will help you establish a work–life balance.

- Let colleagues know you have a new baby: being proud of your new son is not the same as becoming a baby bore.
- Talk to your partner about how the two of you can work together to help you become a great working dad.
- Talk to your employer about any special provision the firm makes for working dads.
- Prepare yourself for the 'family business stays out of the workplace' culture that still exists in some (less enlightened) workplaces.
- Remember that whatever your work situation, you always have options.
- Be prepared to mess it up sometimes and be ready to apologise when you do (having the local florist's number on speed dial could be handy).

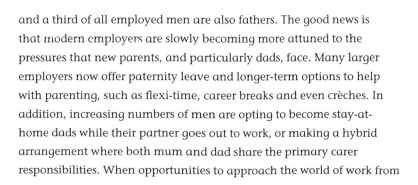

and a third of all employed men are also fathers. The good news is that modern employers are slowly becoming more attuned to the pressures that new parents, and particularly dads, face. Many larger employers now offer paternity leave and longer-term options to help with parenting, such as flexi-time, career breaks and even crèches. In addition, increasing numbers of men are opting to become stay-at-home dads while their partner goes out to work, or making a hybrid arrangement where both mum and dad share the primary carer responsibilities. When opportunities to approach the world of work from

a different angle do exist, take some time to consider what your priorities are. As you get back into the swing of the world of work, make sure you talk with your partner about the things that are important to you both. How important is your career? How important is hers? How much do you need to earn as a family? How important is being at home with your child, both to you and to her? Agreeing your priorities together, within the limitation of what is practically possible, can be a major step towards getting the balance right.

Don't be too quick to assume that you should automatically carry on working full-time, flat out. Recent research that shows just how important a dad's influence is. Children whose dads were actively involved in their lives achieved higher academically, had greater problem-solving abilities and suffered fewer mental health problems than children who lacked a dad's involvement. They also showed more empathy, had greater self-control and less stereotyped beliefs about men and women, which may account for the fact that they also went on to have more solid marriages later in life. So don't underestimate the value of time spent at home with your child.

It's like riding a bike

Finding a good work–life balance is a bit like learning to ride a bike. You'll probably remember lurching from one side to the other as you first set off on your own and struggled to find a balance. In a similar way, it's difficult to find and establish a balance between work and home life that works for you, your partner and your child. You might have to take some risks (such as talking to your boss about flexible working, or asking to work part-time) and you may suffer occasional wobbles, but the main thing is to keep a goal in mind and keep trying. If you have a good relationship with

> Monday morning… Already?
> Just five more minutezzzzzz…
> #needmoresleep

your employer, talk over your thinking with them and see if there is any flexibility in working arrangements, even over the short term – there may be more room to change working arrangements than you think.

See the funny side

Whatever happens, never lose your sense of humour; it will keep things in perspective, prevent tense relationships getting out of hand and boost your morale. Sometimes it will take your partner to help you see the funny side of the times you turned up for a meeting with baby cereal stuck to your ear, vomit down your back, or carrying a dirty nappy in your pocket. Laughing together may not solve every challenge you face, but it will make you feel better equipped to overcome them.

Condensed idea
You can't avoid the tensions of striking a work–life balance, but you can navigate the transition successfully

41 Smarter at home

When you're juggling work and family life, you need to work smarter at your job and at home. There's no need to give your baby a scheduling app (tempting!), but organizing your home life with the same attention that you give to your work can reap quick dividends.

You're their one and only

Let's face it, most dads are used to organizing their working day with the precision of a well-oiled machine. If we make an appointment, we make sure we keep it. We work to deadlines, even though we may cut them fine. We make decisions and we stick to them. At the same time however, many of us would also confess that we take a rather different approach to home life. We're tempted to make more casual arrangements – 'I'll get there if I can', 'Perhaps I'll see you there', 'Don't expect me until late' kind of thing. This is fine when it's just you and your partner, adult to adult: after all, how you arrange your relationship and social life is entirely up to you.

Now, however, your situation is different. You're a dad, and that means you play a central role in a new family of three. This isn't a role you can dip in and out of; while we all like to feel indispensable at work, you really are indispensable at home, where you're the one and only dad. It's vital to get priorities right straight from the start, because while the price you pay for 'inefficiency' at home may be less tangible, it's arguably far greater. Does it really matter if you don't quite make it home for bathtime or bedtime? Well of course it doesn't – occasionally. But your absence will be felt and feelings will be hurt. If you do it too often, they'll stop expecting you to be there, and your role in your child's life will shrink alongside your physical absence.

Go home to work

For most of us, it's not a lack of love that causes us to fail on home commitments, it's more a lack of organization. The challenge for every new dad, therefore, is to learn to work smarter at home. Now's the time to discard the casual approach to your family calendar and begin to apply the principles from your job in your home life too. Send an unequivocal message to your child and partner: show them that they are high enough on your list of priorities to put them in your diary first. Your planning needn't quite reach diary entries like this: '6.30 p.m. bath and baby to bed; 8.30 p.m. talk to partner; 9.30 p.m. sex'; but literally booking time in your diary for your home life does makes sense. You might want to tag an hour with a reminder to 'leave on time', 'keep free', or 'stay in'. If you don't block out time to recharge and hang out with them, it may barely ever happen. Physically writing or keying it in will remind you that, actually, this is not free time. You're busy – being a dad and a partner.

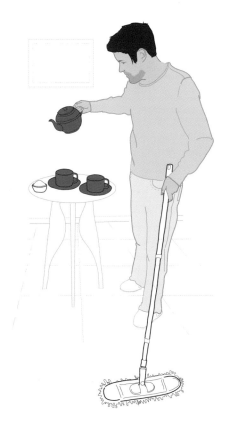

You may think this talk of diaries seems a little excessive. You might work locally, with no unsocial hours and no need to take work home. I'd urge you to follow the principle anyway. In the not-too-distant future your son will be booking you into his diary, not the other way the round. If you have a job that takes you away from home, ensure that when you're back, you put in the effort. Help your family to know that they are number one priority for you, the very centre of your life.

Get organized

If you know that work pressures are likely to bite, talk to your partner about setting a routine in place. Agree that on certain days you might work late, but on others you'll definitely be home on time. If you have to stay late unexpectedly, trade this for another 'early day'. When it arrives, make sure you're home on time, ready to pitch in. Come home ready

Don't trip over the washing

It's great to be able to put your feet up at the end of the day, safe in the knowledge that you've imparted your time and manly wisdom to your firstborn and tuned your emotional intelligence to your partner's cares and concerns. You even bought home a takeaway curry for you both. You've every right to feel pleased with yourself. Just make sure you're seeing the even bigger picture too. I'm talking the 'H' word here. Although we're all marching into the third millennium, proudly wearing our 'modern man' pin badges, when it comes to housework many of us still have to be asked to join in.

If you've put the washing on once, don't put it on your social network page and wait for the 'likes' to pour in. This is a chore that needs doing daily. If you are expecting some kind of brownie points, reward or recognition for cleaning the bathroom once in a while, think again. Are you doing this five or 50 per cent of the time? If you're on five, she's on 95. It might be time to start facing up to the fact that you're going to have to start pulling your weight with domestic chores as well as childcare. Look on the bright side though: the effect on your partner can be stratospheric. Pull on the Marigolds and step back. You've never looked so hot.

to work at being a dad. Remember too that communication is a two-way street and always keep your partner in the mix. Besides listening to what's been going on in your partner's day, talk to her about what's going on for you at work too. It will help her to feel less distanced from your 'other life', and will help smooth the way if you do have to do some work when you are home. If

> No one ever said 'I wish I'd spent more time at the office' as they were dying. #wiserview

or when your partner returns to work, you'll need to set time aside each week to talk about each other's schedules, so why not start now? Initially your two schedules may look very different, but you'll feel more in touch with each other's lives and less vulnerable to surprises when you compare them.

As much as you are able to, adopt a 'play now, work later' attitude. Switch off your work emails and phones when you're at home at home; in reality, very few issues need instant attention. If you simply have to be in touch, avoid checking emails until after your baby has gone to sleep and your partner is taking a great-smelling soak in the bath.

Baby Buddhas

Finally, enjoy the benefits. You may have had a total bummer of a day at work. The boss was in a foul mood, nothing worked out the way you'd planned, the journey home was a nightmare. Sit with your baby for a while. Watch him sleep, listen to him breathe. Slowly, gradually, the stresses of the day will simply fade away.

Condensed idea
Getting organized at home shows your family where your priorities lie

Work less

Research shows that men tend to work longer hours when their first child is born. For some, it's the result of feeling a new financial responsibility; others confess that it's easier to stay at work than deal with the controlled chaos of the baby's bedtime routine at home.

Do you have to work this hard?

It's tempting to believe that, one day, we will all be so established in our work that we'll be free to spend more time with our kids. But for now, lots of dads feel they have to work hard because they want to give their kids 'the best' – to maintain a standard of living to which, as my friend Joe says, his own kids 'are rapidly becoming accustomed'. On the face of it, this seems a reasonable, generous aim for any dad. As we've seen elsewhere in this book, kids don't come cheap.

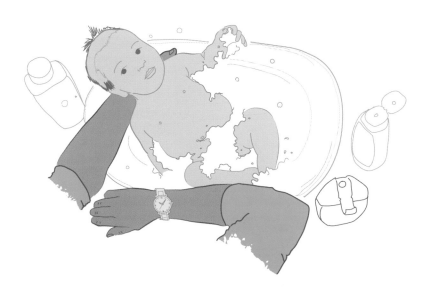

However, while we all have to work late sometimes – the pressure's on, something needs finishing, or a crisis has occurred – try to avoid this becoming a regular thing. The odd half an hour here or hour there can start to add up to several times a week, and before you know it, working late can almost become a habit.

As you become accustomed to being a parent, ask yourself whether there are times when you don't really need to work late, but have just become used to doing so? If so, it's worth telling yourself simply to go home. Working late is an ever-increasing part of our culture, but many successful businessmen and captains of industry have reached positions of influence without compromising their role as fathers. And in any case, at the end of the day, which is really the more important?

Work-related socializing

This one's tricky. No one would suggest that you cut out all of your work social life; after all, it's an important part of working in a team and many a deal has been struck over a drink after work. In the first few weeks and months in particular, however, keep these engagements to a minimum. Allow a good habit to develop by positively opting to go home more often than not.

If you do often work late, and especially if the habit has crept up on you since your child was born, you might want to think about why this is happening. It's just possible that you're avoiding something. Some dads worry about dropping their baby in the bath – to such an extent that they'd rather not bath them at all. Others have broader concerns, perhaps feeling uncomfortable with their role as dad in general; they may feel more comfortable as a salesman, businessman or lawyer – whatever identity they have at work. If you find yourself wanting to work late regularly, this might be a good time to call on other new dads or men who are further along the line than you are (see pages 156–59) and talk it over. Don't let this wonderful relationship slip away because of unfounded fears.

Set boundaries

The prevalence of home computers and Internet connections means that many of us now work from home in the evenings, even after being 'away' at work all day. However, your new responsibilities as a dad mean that you have to practise what might be a new skill: saying no. Decide with your partner what is a reasonable level of work intrusion and work hard to recognize when something oversteps this boundary. Don't be surprised if she gently reminds you, from time to time, of your agreement.

This is not a foolproof method: you won't always have much choice about whether you have to do something out of hours, and neither is it an excuse to be difficult or uncooperative. In fact you'll have to work extra efficiently within your normal hours to pull it off successfully. Regard it as a benchmark instead. If a colleague wants to call you at 7.30 in the evening just as you know you'll be putting your son to bed, don't automatically agree – suggest an alternative. If you give the impression that you're always available, people will expect you to be. You'll also be teaching your child useful negotiating and assertiveness skills that will be very useful to him as he grows older.

> All work and no play makes me a very dull dad indeed.
> #worktolivenotlivetowork

Leave work at work

Make sure that people at work know your family is a big priority for you. You needn't raise it at every staff meeting or annual appraisal, but be clear that your family will always be your first concern. Over time it will begin to drip feed into your work colleagues' perspective of what is reasonable to expect from you. Ultimately you'll earn the respect of your workmates and well as your partner and, over time, your growing child.

Flexible working

Technology and different ways of working mean that increasing numbers of men are taking a more flexible approach to their jobs. Virtual working, compressed hours, flexi-time and a myriad of other creative solutions are appearing on the table for the modern working dad. If you'd like to pursue the option of working flexibly, you'll need to gain your employer's approval.

- Be realistic. Make sure that what you're asking for fits in appropriately with the job you do and the business you're in.
- Be informed. Find out if other people in comparable roles already work in a similar way.
- Be clear. Write down what you want – it will clarify your thinking and help you to shape a considered case.
- Be professional. A corridor chat won't give your boss the impression that you're serious about your proposal.
- Be positive. Put yourself in your employer's shoes, helping the firm to say yes to your proposals by identifying potential problems and offering solutions. Put forward a strong business case that sells the benefits.
- Be flexible. Be prepared to consider alternative, creative options.
- Be good. A positive response is going to be more likely if you're already considered a conscientious worker.

Condensed idea
Making positive choices at work will help to keep family your priority

(43) Being there

In today's fast-moving world, we're bombarded with information and the opportunities for distraction are enormous. You might need to be especially disciplined in carving out proper time for your baby to make sure that when you're with her you're really with her.

No regrets

You've probably heard the story of the tough but successful lawyer who, on his deathbed, was asked whether he'd do anything differently if he had the chance to live his life over again. The story goes that he replied, 'I'd eat more ice cream, ride more rollercoasters and...' (add your own version of his response here). The story itself may be apocryphal, but the point it makes is clear and true. We need to make the time to, well, live. Really experience all the extraordinary things that life has to offer, rather than simply exist. As life crowds in with competing demands and conflicting priorities, it's easy to let days, weeks and even years go by in something of a blur. Do you ever find yourself thinking that you'd love to have more time for the important things, but it's just that the urgent things keep coming up?

> Just found a raisin stuck to my smartphone. Ate it, obviously. #bizarrefruitsalad

Here's the thing: not being around for our kids at the right time is one of the commonest and biggest mistakes we dads make. Most of us order our priorities on the assumption that we'll be around for many years to come but – difficult as it is to grasp right now – your daughter's childhood will whizz past a lot sooner than you think. No one's wishing time away, but the clock is ticking. If you think about it, there aren't all that many summer holidays, Christmas Eves, Bonfire nights, Thanksgivings and Halloweens in a single childhood. So make sure you're really there, paying attention. These are unrepeatable moments.

Here but not here

As your child grows up, recognize from early on that being 'around' for your partner and baby isn't necessarily the same as really being there. Physically being in a space isn't the same as being connected to the world and people around

you, and connection is the name of the game. Start to notice the things that distract your attention. There's the TV, for example, which you can continue to watch while half-listening to your partner telling you about her day. In a few years' time, you can half-listen to your daughter's day too. At least they'll have your full concentration in the ad breaks, eh? And let's talk about phones. Or your computer. Or the two put together in a smartphone. Now we've got a wonderful universe of distraction right there in our pockets.

Don't get me wrong, a little distraction can sometimes be exactly what you need after a hard day. I love watching a hilarious video of a cat with scary eyes dancing on a piano as much as the next man. You may be partial to getting the low down on what friends and acquaintances have

10 ways to switch off

- Don't always pick up the phone when it rings. The caller can leave a message or ring back if it's urgent.
- Keep your phone in a particular place in your home, not always in your pocket.
- Don't keep your phone by the bed.
- Ask yourself if you really need to check your emails/social network updates this very minute.
- Get some exercise with your partner and child. Leave your phone at home.
- Limit your own screen time each day.
- Have a screen-free evening once (preferably twice) a week – including phones, computers, ereaders and TVs.
- Have a TV-free week, once every two months.
- Only watch TV when your favourite programmes are showing.
- Buy a cheap 'calls and text only' phone to use at weekends. It'll stop you checking your emails or browsing every 5 minutes.

been up to in their online life, but whatever your poison, it's the balance that matters. We've all held a conversation while simultaneously checking our text messages, but the warnings bells should sound when this multi-tasking begins to characterize our interactions with everyone.

Watch the dads in a café on a Saturday morning if you don't believe me. They're 'with' their kids, but their attention is almost entirely on their phones as they're checking, texting, emailing and gaming. They are physically present and switched on, but virtually oblivious to the words, actions and feelings of those around them.

Make sure you never inadvertently 'multi-task' your daughter and partner in the same way, never fully being 'with' them. They deserve much more from you. I'm not suggesting it will be easy. On some occasions, in fact, it will take a real force of will, but ask your partner to keep you in check. After all, to help you be the best dad you can be, she and the baby need an engaged you. They need to know you're there.

A wise investment

At the moment, your daughter's still tiny. You're just getting to know her and she's just getting to know you too. Boy, oh boy, you've got some great times ahead. One day, though, when she's older, someone, somewhere is going to ask her an important question when you're not there. Not an important question for her perhaps, but certainly an important one for you. Someone will ask her, 'What's your dad like?'

Your daughter will probably ponder for a moment or so before giving her response. When she does finally speak, though, she'll be delivering a verdict of sorts. It'll be the shorthand version of course, with all the details removed, but her reply will offer her interpretation of your efforts as a dad – beyond the first few weeks, beyond the first few years, maybe even beyond the first few decades – in just a few sentences.

It'll be the things that really struck home for her; the things that seemed important to you. Now is the time to begin making sure that the answer she gives is one of which you, and she, can be rightly proud. Now's the time to ensure that whatever other comment she chooses to make, she'll also say, 'He's always there for me.'

Condensed idea
Put down the phone, step away from the computer, and look at your gorgeous family instead

44 Let go of the guilt

It's often said that guilt is an inevitable part of a parent's job description. As you begin to find your way on the work–life balance, there will be times when you feel the pinch. If you find yourself wishfully thinking for superpowers, drop the guilt and be realistic.

Two places at once

One favourite topic of conversation amongst the kids in our house starts with the question: 'What's your favourite superpower?' Obviously none of us have any superpowers, so it's not actually a matter of choosing the ones we like the best from our vast household armoury of lasers, force fields, super strength and freeze rays. It's more of a 'what superpower would you have if you could have one?' conversation. Flying is up there, obviously. Invisibility is always high on the list. Whenever I'm asked the question – which is much more regularly than you might expect – I try to use it to inject a bit of fatherly wisdom, benevolently creating an 'important learning opportunity' for the children. 'I'd like to have the power of always knowing the answer,' I say. 'Leading the charge to solve world hunger, poverty, wars and man's inhumanity to man'. I ignore my wife's mutterings that, never mind the superpower, I seem to be of the opinion that I'm always right already.

To be honest though, there is one superpower I'd really appreciate: the ability to be in more than one place at the same time. A clone or two of myself would be dead handy. One of me could be an expert in housework, cooking and gardening; another could do some kind of paid work; and a third could devote his time entirely to the kids. The trouble is, back in the real world, there is only one of me. There's only one of you too; spread, I'd hazard a guess, all too thinly over the competing demands that are made of you. Without those superpowers, you can't be in more than one place at a time.

Returning to work after the birth of your baby really drives the point home and it's easy to end up burdened by emotional guilt as a result. Guilt that you're not there for your child when you should be, guilt that you're not supporting your partner enough, guilt that you're not giving all that you can to your job, and frustration that you're not really even there for yourself. Guilt is probably always going to appear somewhere on a working dad's job description, but there are things that you can do to make a difference to the way you feel.

Legitimate and illegitimate guilt

Success as a working dad begins by recognizing that there are two kinds of guilt: legitimate and illegitimate. It's vital to learn to tell the difference. Legitimate guilt is basically where it's a fair cop – it's the guilt you feel, for example, if you've ever driven home late, just a tad over the speed limit, and a police car pulls out behind you, flashing its lights. In your working life, although it's tough at the time, legitimate guilt can be

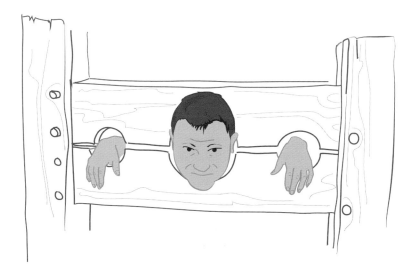

a real friend, alerting you to issues you need to deal with. If you realize that you're consistently making choices at work that result in keeping you away from your family – the people who need you most – you probably should feel guilty. Don't squash it or ignore it. Deal with it. Use it as the motivation to do something positive and make some changes.

The second type of guilt is almost more important to recognize because it's the type that many of us suffer from a lot of the time. Illegitimate guilt is the vague, nebulous, nagging feeling that's difficult to pin

There is a always a way back

New mums and dads can spend an unnecessary amount of time in a state of emotional angst. Some of us seem almost to thrive on the guilt as we ponder all the ways we let out kids down: missing the night-time bath, forgetting the goodnight kiss or forgetting to play dollies 'later on' even though we'd promised.

There's a great truth, however, which is good to keep in mind as your child grows up. He wants this parenting business to work out just as you much as you do. He has an inbuilt compulsion to love you as his dad and to make your relationship work. While you fumble along in the detail, he'll be looking at the big picture. He'll forgive your failings because he can see that you're just doing your best – doing your utmost to be a dad who is there for him, supporting him, spending time with him and willing him on. Even when you mess up, there will always be a way back. Ask for forgiveness when you need to, and be ready to accept it too. Notice the guilt if it's useful, then forgive yourself and move on. Tomorrow is another day.

down but eats away at us anyway. Picture that scene again, where you're driving home and a police car pulls out behind you. You're not speeding, you're driving carefully, all your lights are working and you've not been drinking. You're doing nothing wrong, yet somehow you still feel guilty. That's illegitimate guilt. It's part of the human psyche;

> DM @Sophie. Sorry I'm late. Waiting for the bus. It's raining. Will make it up. xx #rushingdad

you know it's dumb, but you can't help feeling it. No matter how conscientious you are as a dad, there will be times when you have to make choices that will leave you with a gnawing sense of unease. When this happens, take the time to talk to your partner, or another dad, and think about the driving force that's making you feel the way you do. Are those guilty feelings legitimate or not?

Learn as you go

There's old adage that goes something like, 'Good decisions are the result of wisdom; wisdom is the result of experience; experience is the result of bad decisions'. Failure isn't the same as making mistakes – we all do that. It's when we give up instead of learning from our previous, poorer decisions and moving on. As a new dad, it's early days and everything's still to play for. Don't be too harsh with yourself about your errors of judgement in balancing your work with being a father and partner. Adopt a more philosophical attitude. Even a big mistake can act as a springboard to getting it right next time.

Condensed idea
Legitimate guilt can propel you into making good choices, but don't feel guilty about things you can't change

45 Unconditional love

From the moment your child is born she will be thrust into a world that demands much from her. The challenge is to give your child a rock-solid foundation of knowing that she's loved – not for what she does, but for who she is. It's what psychologists call 'unconditional love'.

Sweet dreams are made of this

It's good to dream, wondering about how things might be and how you can best make them happen. I would be willing to bet, while you've been getting used to the daunting prospect of impending fatherhood, that there has been an occasion or two when you have taken a moment to contemplate what the future might hold for your son or daughter once he or she finally arrives.

It's clear that you already want the best for your child – if you didn't you wouldn't be reading a book like this one. Perhaps, however, you have other ambitions for them too. You might have found yourself thinking about what your kid may 'turn into' when they grow up: scientist, artist, actor, politician, astronaut? Maybe you can picture them receiving a university degree, scoring the winning goal in an international tennis match or carving out a successful career as an entrepreneur. Or perhaps there's a family profession you would like your son or daughter to follow.

Fundamentally, though, if you ask 99.9 percent of dads – and mums for that matter – what they really want for their child, their answer can be captured in a simple statement: 'I want them to be happy'. Your definition of what it means to be happy will shape and colour your child's entire life, so it's vital to get it right.

No strings attached

Close your eyes and think for a moment. How many people in your life can you say have truly loved you unconditionally? Loved without condition – loved with no strings attached? Go on. Really think. Count them up – true, uncomplicated, unconditional love.

I have done this exercise with many hundreds of mums and dads over the years and the response has always been the same. Most people can point to, at most, one or two people who have consistently, unflaggingly, unconditionally loved them. And who do you think these loving people were? Have a guess.

Making your way in the world is not always an easy business. From the moment a child is born he is thrust into a competitive environment where, just like you, he will find himself accepted or rejected on the basis of how he performs. It's a tough lesson to learn but it's one we're all familiar with. The harsh reality is that some people will have time, or not, for your precious son or daughter because of what he or she can offer or deliver to them, such as contacts or expertise. They will judge your child largely on the strength of what he or she is doing, or can do.

As parents, our task is to be the exception to this rule. We have a different role to play compared to the rest of the world. As dads, we need to love our kids, not for what they can achieve, but for who they are. No strings attached.

You can prepare for this kind of relationship before your child is born by being involved and interested in your partner's pregnancy. Once the baby is born, embrace fatherhood; play, hold and talk to your baby, so he has clear signs of your love. It's not enough just to feel it – you need to make sure he knows it. Send a clear, emphatic and unequivocal message from the very start: 'I want to be your father. I am interested in you and I enjoy being with you. You and I have a relationship that is vitally important to me. The world is a better place simply because it has you in it'.

How to love and be loved

Keep in mind that happiness comes from a sense of knowing that you are loved, no matter what you do.

- Be alert to your own expectations for your children even from the earliest days. Don't inadvertently send the message that your love for them is dependent upon their success.
- Get into good habits as soon as your child is born. It's easy to show a small baby that you love him – it may be less straightforward when he's a challenging teenager.
- Words are important but not enough – what you do says more.
- Keep the long game in mind – the foundations you build even in these earliest days can stand your child in good stead for the whole of their life.

Resistant to Knocks

Depending on your generation, you may remember growing up playing with a spinning top or a gyroscope. In the games I played, the idea was to get your top spinning as fast as possible before others tried to knock it over with theirs. We'd spend hour after hour battling away, perfecting our technique. We soon discovered that the faster the spin, the better our tops became at righting themselves and the harder the knocks they could withstand.

> RT @JeanPaulRichter. What a father says to his children is not heard by the world, but it will be heard by posterity. #lovingdad

For me, the image of a spinning top is a great analogy for the unique role of a parent. It is not for us to be perfect, nor to be always right, nor even to be always there – relatively speaking it won't be too long before your son or daughter flies the nest. Instead, it's our job to give our kids the 'spin' they need to withstand the knocks that this world will inevitably give them. Our unconditional love will give our children the strength they need to right themselves when difficult times come along.

The tragedy is that a significant proportion of people feel this didn't happen for them. Indeed, this may be your own experience. You may feel that you were never really good enough for your own parents and ever since you've been playing catch up. So here's your chance to get it right. It's your responsibility to ensure that your child will always know that at least one person loves them, no questions asked.

Condensed idea
Your main task as a dad is to love your child, just as he or she is

46 Love is spelled T-I-M-E

Kids don't look at time in the same way as adults do, living much more 'in the moment'. The more time you spend with your children, particularly in the early years, the better your relationship will be. They know that you spend time on the things you love.

Building a lasting bond

Cast your mind back to when you and your partner first got together; the time when your fledgling relationship became a little more serious. The romantic walks together, phone calls, little loving texts and the staying up until the small hours of the morning just talking. Each time you parted, your thoughts turned to when you'd see her again. All over the world young lovers are 'busy doing nothing' together, just for the pleasure of spending time with the person they love.

Right now you're in the same fledgling stage of your relationship with your baby. You'll only get to know each other by hanging out together. And this holds true for his whole life. As he grows up to be a toddler, then goes to school, he will continue to make the connection between the time you spend with him and the way you feel about him. Sometimes all that will be required is for you to be there in the room while he plays. At other times, you'll need to be more actively involved in what he's doing. All toddlers are 'attention junkies', and yours will be an expert at finding ever more ingenious ways to get your attention more often.

Like it or not, your child will judge how important he is to you on the quantity and quality of time you spend with him. It sounds harsh, but it makes a lot of sense. After all, when you love someone, you want to spend as much time with them as you can. It's true for babies, it's true for toddlers, it's true for teenagers and it's true for adults. We all spell love T-I-M-E. Our self-esteem gets a boost when someone we love sends us the message, 'I like being with you. This is where I want to be.'

Forget quality time

Kids can teach us a lot about how to view time positively. As adults, we can often find ourselves saying to other people, 'I'm here, but I've only got five minutes', whereas to a small child five minutes presents a wealth of opportunity. Five minutes? That's tons of time! Play with me!

Keep calm and carry on reading

Babies and children love books. You may not be much of a reader yourself, but even from the earliest days, reading to your child is a great thing to do. For a start, it gives you a reason to spend time with your baby and even gives you things to say. Let's face it, you don't get too much conversation from a six-month-old and even the most creative dad can run dry after a while.

More importantly though, reading helps them to get used to hearing the tone of your voice (much like they did in the womb) and it helps you to switch off from the stresses of an adult day. Better still, it'll help him with his language development, building his vocabulary and encouraging his imagination – all important skills for later life. Most of all, it'll give you some special time one on one. Keep reading together as he grows up and make it a tradition for you and your son.

No child will recognize the concept of 'quality time' so often used by us adults. We say things like 'I'm looking forward to spending a bit of quality time with the family this weekend' or 'a bit of quality time with my partner'. The phrase has passed so much into our common parlance that we rarely ever question what it really means.

There are a couple of problems with the 'quality time' idea, however. Firstly, it presupposes that we can decide when we are available to have 'quality time' with someone else, without really taking into account whether it works for them or not. Secondly, it automatically assumes that the time itself will be of good quality when it finally comes. There's nothing like the arrival of a child on the scene to put this into perspective. You might have had their bedtime story scheduled on your calendar for a fortnight or so, but when it comes to it, your son might be grumpy, tired or already fast asleep. You're ready, but he's not. Scroll forward a decade or so and having replied to your subtle enquiries about 'How are things going?' with a nondescript 'Fine...', you might later find your son appearing at your bedroom door at midnight because now is the time he really wants to talk. Making yourself available when it really counts is what really matters.

> Off to have a chat with junior.
> #hangingoutwiththefamily

Don't get me wrong here; no one's suggesting that whenever your baby, toddler, eight-year-old or teenager calls you, you must automatically come running. There are boundaries and you have responsibilities elsewhere too. You may not live with the mother of your child and so your domestic circumstances may mean that you're unable to spend as much time with him as you'd like to. The important thing is to understand the value in shifting your perspective to that of your child's. Get your priorities right and do what you can. The greater quantity of time you can give to your child, whatever their age, the more chance you'll have of getting some real quality somewhere within it.

Start building memories now

If you think about your best childhood memory, I bet it won't be about
an object – perhaps a present you received after weeks of nagging your
parents. Instead, it's more likely to be about a time you spent with your
mum or dad doing something that meant a lot to you. A funny incident,
a happy period, a particular occasion. Keep this in mind as your child
grows up. Avoid the temptation to confuse 'Love is spelled T-I-M-E' with
a different spelling: 'G-I-F-T'. Children quickly learn that gifts tend
to make an appearance when time is in short supply, and they feel
short-changed, because it's you they want. It is important to know that
expensive holidays and presents make little difference to a child. He'd
trade them all in a second for more time with you.

Condensed idea
Kids feel the time you spend with them
as an expression of love

47 Five things I wish I'd known

Every dad has something to learn from another; not just about babies, but about fatherhood in general. The themes may sound familiar but many men admit that they never fully appreciated the true meaning of these wise words until they became a father themselves.

Time goes quickly

When it comes to parenthood, there really is no time to waste. Becoming a father is like stepping into a time machine and pressing fast forward on the flux capacitor. Without wanting to risk sounding like a grandfather here (I'm not one, by the way!), father after father is amazed at how quickly the years rush by. It's easy to picture long years ahead to hang out with your daughter before she finally grows up and flies the nest, but in reality she'll be leaving home much sooner than you think. Not in a physical way, perhaps, but her mental orientation will begin to shift towards the big wide world out there from quite early on. Compare, for example, the responses you'd get from a 15-year-old, compared to those she'd make some six years earlier, if you suggested that she hang out with you rather than with her mates. A wise friend said to me once that you should think of parenthood from day one as preparation for letting your children go. Cherish your time with your child now; it's so precious, and so much shorter than you think.

> For the rest of today, I'm going to be an error-free zone. It's 23:37, but I still think I can do it.
> #alwaysoptimistic

Small things count

In fatherhood, every moment and every little touch counts. Making sure you carve out even a small snippet of time with your partner each day really will make a difference to how you feel towards each other. Similarly, staying engaged with your child will help you to seize the moment when she needs to tell you something important, because in all likelihood it will tumble out while you're both doing something else together. Big moments tend to happen when you least expect them, so make sure that your child's 'small voice' doesn't get lost in your busy day.

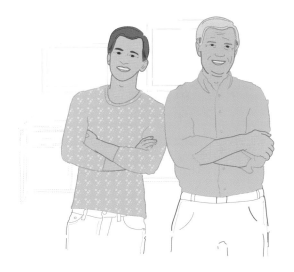

Taking time to appreciate and enjoy the little things that your children do and say can be extremely rewarding. Take a moment to be kind to them; be generous with your time and words. Think of something to say that will make them feel good. Even on the busiest of days, stand still with your partner and child for a few moments and allow yourself to become consciously aware of how much you love them. They will notice and all of you will benefit enormously.

Love conquers all

Many dads are caught off guard by the sheer intensity of the love they feel for their child. It might take a little while to get going at the beginning, but as every day goes by be prepared for the ache as your heart grows bigger and fuller. Make sure she knows it. Never stop telling her how much you love her and never stop showing her either. Even when she's as tall as you, she'll still appreciate hearing it. Put it at the heart of your fatherhood and it'll become part of who she is too. When you're angry, show her you love her. When you're upset, show her you love her. Catch her by surprise and show her you love her. Loving her unconditionally – don't make it relate only to times when she does well, or achieves something. This will only result in your daughter thinking that you only love her if she is successful, and that if she fails at something, she will lose your love. Love her whatever and whenever, and tell her you love her as often as you can.

Your child will be like you

We all say it, but it really is true. One day your child will be like you. Not an exact copy, but certainly a good impression. Just wait for the moment that you hear your words come out of her mouth. The power of being a role model brings with it an awesome responsibility. Show your daughter what's important. To paraphrase US author Clarence Kelland's famous quote, 'Live and let her watch you do it'. Act your age and let her act hers. Be the grown-up in the relationship. She might have a strop occasionally, throw herself onto the floor and scream until she's blue in the face (at pretty much any age). However much you may feel like losing your temper and acting the same way as your child, you can't. Show her instead what a patient, self-controlled, loving father looks like, because you're modelling her future.

You are not a back-up parent

Sometimes society struggles to pinpoint a man's exact parental role from the moment his child is conceived to the day she leaves home. To combat this, remember that you are not a sub-standard mum. Be informed, involved and engaged – your child needs you. Spark her imagination; give her your time; get your hands dirty. Never regard anything as 'only for mums', but share the load instead. You're a fantastic first-time father after all. You're a full, equal partner in raising your child to be a fully-fledged, all-singing, all-dancing member of the human race.

'I didn't expect that!'

Here are 10 of the most surprising facts about fatherhood.

- You'll need to pack the same amount of stuff for an overnight stay as you will for a three-week holiday.
- Time stands still when walking with a toddler. Every piece of litter, chewing gum, bird dropping and leaf must be closely inspected.
- Eventually every coat pocket will hold at least one small box of raisins.
- Strategically positioned bits of apple can do untold damage to anything technological.
- One day you'll listen to sing-along songs even when the kids aren't in the car.
- They'll want to join you in the toilet when you're having a bit of a 'ponder'.
- Your kids will positively love being naked. Anywhere. Anytime.
- You'll disgust yourself as you shove your baby's half-chewed banana into your mouth just because you're not near a bin.
- The inside of your car will resemble a skip.
- A baby can find a remote control, however well you've hidden it.

Condensed idea
Years are going to pass in a flash, so catch the minutes and use them well

48 Four rules to happiness

With all this focus on fathers, it's easy to take the spotlight off the person who really has played the biggest part in the life of your baby so far. The role your partner plays is extraordinary, and supporting her through the early days is of paramount importance.

Before we get started

Just a few words of warning to start with. First, I realize that knowing nothing about your domestic situation does not put me in the strongest position for knowing the ins and outs of what particular support your very own partner is looking for from you. Secondly, I don't want to inadvertently sound chauvinistic or gender biased, so forgive me if I do. Who takes on which roles in your home is down to each particular couple. Finally – and this is the big one – what follows here might, on the face of it, sound a bit basic. Do you, for example, really need the concept of helping out around the house occasionally set out for you in black and white? Unfortunately, if I and the dads I know are anything to go by, yes, you probably do. Giving the best to the mothers of our kids as they themselves adjust to parenthood means getting the basics right. So, that said, here we go.

1: Think for yourself

Don't wait to be asked to do the things that deep down you know you need to do. Seize the initiative. It really isn't rocket science – if you see something that needs doing, do it. When your baby's nappy needs changing for the fifth time, get on with it (without the precursory 'I did it last time' conversation). Use it as an excuse for a bit of one-to-one bonding time with your child – you'll always be glad you did. Arrive

10 things best left unsaid

I know I don't really have to tell you, but just in case, here are 10 things worth keeping your trap shut about. Play 'foot in mouth bingo' and see how often you nearly say it.

- What time do you think we might eat?
- Why is the baby crying?
- It's your turn.
- You're just like your mother/my mother.
- Pregnancy's not an illness, you know.
- Blimey, you look knackered.
- Stop getting so emotional.
- 'So and so' looks fantastic. You'd never think she'd had a baby at the same time as you.
- So when will you be in the mood?
- It's all right for you; I've got to get up for work in the morning.

home early, unexpectedly, now and then, just to give your partner a break. Be the one who makes the tea in the morning (unless you've managed to sneak a pre-arranged lie-in one day), without having to be asked. I know it's a cliché, but it really is the thought that counts: even more than the deed itself.

2: Look around you

One of my sons isn't the tidiest person in the world. From time to time, my partner and I put on protective clothing and do a cleaning raid on his bedroom, just to reduce the risk of biological contamination for the rest of the street. The strange thing is, he's never very resistant to helping with tidying up from time to time. It's more that he genuinely can't see the need. Unfortunately, he's not the only one. Items left at the foot of the stairs to 'go up' and baskets of dirty laundry (even strategically positioned by my wife in front of the washing machine) somehow become magically invisible to me. I'm happy to help when prodded, but I don't always spot what needs doing.

As Team Parent swings into action, put yourself in your partner's shoes. Try to see things differently. If you don't know what needs doing, ask. In the meantime, put this book down and go and clean the house. If you don't know how the washing machine works, find out. Don't just offer to make dinner, make the dinner. If cooking's never really been your thing, find a small range of simple, healthy meals that you can rustle up – it will work wonders. You don't have to be flash. It's about working as a team and easing the burden for your partner. And by the way, there's nothing more romantic, so I'm told, than a surprise basket of clean washing, a spontaneously emptied dishwasher or a miraculously sparkling toilet!

3: Listen

Many new mums say that one of the unexpected struggles of early parenthood is the sense of isolation. Your partner will be able to go out to see her friends with the baby, of course, but the actual getting out will be hard work. And most of her friends may be non-parents, which means they're not at

> Big foot. Large mouth. Bang! Straight in.
> #emotionalintelligencebypass

home during the day. This means that on plenty of days, it'll be just her and the baby at home. No proper adult conversation over the course of an entire day is hard if you're a social being, and looking after a small child can seem like the performance of endless routines at times. She'll be attuned to the mundanities herself, but when you get in from your day, she'll need to talk to you about them anyway. Be ready to switch on, not switch off. Get ready to listen.

4: Be loving

Always remember the power of your words. Remind yourself constantly. Use them to build your partner up, not knock her down. Avoid sliding into conversations that begin 'You always…(do this)' or 'You never…(do that)'. Parenthood is not a competition about who is the most tired or who's got the hardest day ahead. When you catch yourself doing it (see box on page 193), say you're sorry. Use your energy instead to invest in the person with whom you decided to have a child. Tell her you love her; tell her you're proud of her; tell her she's great, and tell her often.

Condensed idea
Help your partner be a fantastic mum and enjoy it

(49) Four things kids need to hear

Fatherhood is all about raising children to be ready for the big wide world. To do this successfully you'll need to continually and relentlessly drip-feed them the key messages that will help them thrive on the road ahead. It's never too early to start.

'I love you'

My wife always tells me that she's a better driver than me because she passed her driving test second time around. Her logic is that she used the first test failure to learn, which puts her above me, the 'more complacent first timer', who just breezed through. Obviously, like every man, I think my driving is fantastic. Deep down, though, I suspect that the difference between the fact that I passed first time and my wife didn't wasn't really down to driving, but something more basic altogether.

Driving instructors make a point of saying that, when it comes to your test, you should exaggerate the movements you make so that the examiner, head in clipboard, can see you making them. You should move your head so that he or she can see you looking in your mirror, looking both ways, checking for other road users. It's not enough just to do the right thing: you have to be seen to do the right thing. Needless to say, I made sure my head movements were so pronounced that the examiner thought I was wearing a neck brace.

Something similar is required when you become a dad. A transformation occurs: gone are the days when life was all about you. Now it's all about your child, your partner and you. However, while the change is enormous for you, it is an internal transformation. As your child grows

Even when appearing as fruit in the school play, children can't hide the fact that it's your face and your approval that they're looking for

up it'll be easy to assume that just because you know that you'd do anything for your son, that you love him with every ounce of your being and can't imagine a world without him, that he'll automatically know it too. To a certain extent he will. But recognize, too, that it is your mission to wipe away even the slightest doubt – to exaggerate your 'movements' by telling him, showing him and giving him your time – that you love him. So he knows, in no uncertain terms, his limitless value as a person.

'You're doing great'

In a few years' time you will encounter the wonderful world of first school assemblies, plays and class performances. Nothing fully prepares a dad for the creativity and general weirdness these productions represent: casts of hundreds; nativity plays featuring octopuses, aliens and other creatures of indeterminate origin; and all manner of unusual interpretations of well-known nursery rhymes and stories.

It's not unusual for the entire class to be lined up ready as the audience arrives. The kids won't be concentrating on the play though. Each one will be craning their necks, searching the sea of faces for their mum or dad. Watch your child's face light up when he sees you. But it won't stop there – throughout he'll be looking at you, anxiously seeking your approval. He'll need to know that he's doing well as he delivers his two-word line 45 minutes into the show. More than that, he'll need to know that – regardless of what anyone else thinks – you think he's doing great and you're proud of him. Praise is the miracle tool. When we're told we've done something well, it gives us the confidence to do it again. As your son grows up, regular, genuine specific praise will give him the confidence he needs to try new things and trust his own judgement.

> I've just had the call: 'Can you come and get me but can you wait round the corner?' #taxidad

'It's OK, let's rebuild it'

It's not always going to be plain sailing of course. A key part of your legacy to your son is teaching him how to respond when things don't go according to plan. It may start with the building of a tower of wooden bricks that topples over as the last block goes on, but later in life it may be the ending of a relationship that broke his heart, the exam that went badly, or the job that fell through. In his life there will be things that he puts a lot of work into, only to see them topple in front of his eyes. It's your job to help him see that even when the worst happens it doesn't mean it's the end of the world.

'The door is always open'

One of the greatest gifts a dad can give his child is to provide an open door. From day one, try to foster a relationship where he feels able to sound you out about the things that are important to him. Don't expect

10 things a child wants to hear

- Go on, leave your broccoli.
- Let's watch your TV programme instead of the football.
- Have you ever wondered where babies come from?
- Haven't you done enough school work for one night?
- Are you sure your music won't go louder?
- You've got to go out dressed like that.
- Isn't it time you got a tattoo?
- I wish I had known that at your age.
- The mess in your bedroom is an artistic triumph.
- You can eat as many sweets as you like.

him to come to you with everything, nor always (if ever) to take your advice, but you'll find that your honesty and non-judgemental approach will mean more to him than he'll ever tell you. Many years of a father/son relationship lie ahead and though you'll always love your son, you may not always like what he does. Later in life he will make decisions that you would rather he didn't. As he grows, you'll need to set some boundaries that he won't like either. Never let negative situations reach the stage where he feels like you've 'walked away'. Always be the adult – ready to make the first move to put things right between you. And make sure he knows that he is and always will be at the centre of your life.

Condensed idea
Say 'I love you' whether things are going great or whether you think your child is making a big mistake

50 Growing up together

The first time you became a father must seem like a distant memory – literally a lifetime ago for your baby who is now such a big part of you. As you look forward to a future of fantastic fatherhood, get ready to learn as much from your child as they do from you.

The end of the beginning

It's been quite a journey. It seems like only yesterday that you were contemplating the prospect of becoming a dad and now, here you are, walking the talk. If you've managed to apply even half of the principles covered elsewhere in this book, you've already done a great job. Give yourself a hearty slap on the back and a quick sit down and cup of tea.

There's no doubt that the early weeks and months after becoming a dad really are quite something. They're a learning curve beyond all others – 'part joy, part guerrilla warfare', as we learned on pages 4–7. But now the future beckons. This really is only the beginning of your journey through fatherhood. So in the same way that you may one day wave goodbye to your daughter as she goes to the shops for the first time, embarks on her first holiday with her friends, or leaves for university, there's one final chance to say again the most important themes we've covered so far. Your

> DM@fantasticfirsttimefather.
> **Thanks Dad. You still dance funny but I love you. #importantstuff**

advice to your daughter may focus on 'look both ways' or 'try to eat something other than tuna', and my suggested top 10 'don't forgets' are listed on the next page. In fact, they're not mine, they're the thoughts of all the dads who have contributed to this book. If you remember nothing else from this book, remember these. Cut them out, if you like, and stick them onto the fridge or into your wallet.

Teacher, manager, coach

As your child grows up, be prepared for your role as a dad to change too. Before too long, the 'teacher' phase where your daughter is totally dependent on you to show her the very basics of life will give way to the 'manager' phase. This is the time when you'll feel more like her social secretary as her interaction with other people gets going. It'll be sorting play dates, and getting her to dance classes, art clubs and so on. Sometimes you might even get her there on time! As she reaches the pre-teen and teenage years your role will change again, but more subtly this time. This is more of a coach or mentor role; giving her your tips and insights about making the best of her game, while helping her to learn for herself how to play it. At this stage she'll thrive in the knowledge that you'll always be there cheering her on: not interfering but ready to celebrate the wins and help her pick herself up from the defeats.

Top 10 tips for the fantastic first-time father

- All dads are pioneers: trust your judgment and be yourself.
- Love your partner and love yourself: remember you're a team.
- From day one set up your parent 'satnav' system: keep the end in mind and focus on getting the important things right along the way.
- Wear your L-plates: admit when you don't have all the answers or you've made a mistake, and be ready to work hard and learn as you go.
- Love them unconditionally and tell them even when they're bigger than you.
- Be there for them: show them you love them by making them a priority.
- Choose your battles: set appropriate boundaries but don't stress over little things.
- Teach your kids the way to live by showing them yourself.
- Let them go: prepare them for life by delegating responsibility to them.
- Enjoy the adventure. Keep loving, keep laughing, keep going.

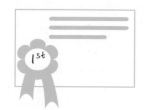

Amidst these changing roles, however, don't expect the learning to be one-way traffic. The funny thing is, and in common with most dads, my own experience of parenthood is that I've learnt much more from my kids than I ever thought possible. It turns out it's a two-way street with more traffic coming towards me than going away. As they get older, I'm realising more and more that they've taught me all the most important things: about love, about selflessness, about priorities and about life.

Let them swim

Every year, hundreds of thousands of mums and dads sign up their children for swimming lessons. As well as it being a fun thing to do, learning to swim is one of the key skills for life. We all know that water can be dangerous and so every parent is faced with two options: keeping their child permanently away from water or teaching them how to swim. The first is exhausting and, frankly, unrealistic. Besides it will deny their kids the glorious joy of flinging themselves headlong into water on a hot day. The choice is clear. Deep down we understand that one of life's most basic yet profound principles is that preparation is the best form of protection.

In exactly the same way, as your daughter grows up into the big wide world she'll one day need to 'swim' for herself. Now's your chance to teach her how to do it, preparing her for the day when you're not there with her. To show her how to keep herself safe but have the freedom to have fun too. The early years of fatherhood are your opportunity to ensure that, when she has to make decisions in the future, your investment in her will help the choices she makes to be good ones.

And finally...

Remember, no one can ever be the mythical perfect father, but you can be a successful, fantastic dad. A father that your child (and you) can be proud of. Your influence may not always be the greatest but it will always be the deepest, and the impact of the way you parent your daughter will ripple down through generations to come. What's more, if you're prepared to put in the effort, it can be the greatest, most rewarding job in the world. So roll up your sleeves, slap on your L-plates and go.

Condensed idea
The best is yet to come

Glossary

Antenatal Before birth; prenatal.

Apgar score The score of a test given one minute and five minutes after birth to assess the baby's skin colour, pulse, reflexes, muscle tone and breathing. A perfect score is 10.

Baby blues Mild depression that develops a few days after giving birth.

Biophysical profile (BPP) An ultrasound test to check foetal breathing, movement and tone, and the volume of amniotic fluid.

Birth plan A parents' list of their preferences for birth management, including preferences for pain relief, induction and so on.

Braxton Hicks contractions 'Practice' contractions that begin around six weeks before birth.

Breech presentation An unusual position of the baby in the uterus, where the baby's bottom or feet face the mother's cervix.

Cerclage A type of stitch performed on a weak or incompetent cervix to keep it closed and prevent a premature birth.

Cervical ripening A process that occurs during early labour, making the cervix soft and thin.

Cervix The narrow, lower end of the uterus that thins and opens during labour.

Caesarean section A surgical procedure in which incisions are made in the abdomen and uterus to deliver a baby. Also called a C-section.

Chorionic villus sampling (CVS) A diagnostic test using placental tissues to screen for genetic abnormalities such as Down's syndrome.

Colostrum A nutrient-rich, sticky yellow fluid secreted by the breasts for the first few days after birth.

Contraction A contraction of the uterine muscle, which tightens the uterus and dilates the cervix.

Crowning The moment during labour when the baby's head can be seen at the vaginal opening.

C-section See caesarean section.

Doula Childbirth assistant who is specially trained to assist mothers during labour and liaise with medical staff.

Down's syndrome A congenital disorder caused by an extra chromosome.

Eclampsia A condition resulting from untreated pre-eclampsia characterized by seizures, very high blood pressure and abnormal blood tests.

Ectopic pregnancy A pregnancy where the fertilized egg has implanted outside the uterus, usually in a Fallopian tube.

Effacement The thinning and softening of the cervix during labour.

Epidural A type of anaesthesia administered into the base of the spine constantly, via a catheter, to numb the lower body.

Episiotomy A surgical incision in the perineum performed to enlarge the vaginal opening during delivery.

Foetal monitoring The monitoring of a baby's heartbeat during labour.

Foetal movement counts A test where women of 27+ weeks gestation count how often their baby moves within an hour.

Foetus The medical name for a baby from 8 weeks of pregnancy until birth.

Fontanelles Soft spots on a baby's head that allow the bony plates of its skull to flex during birth.

Forceps Surgical 'tongs' that are used to help deliver a baby.

Full-term A baby born at 37–42 weeks' gestation.

Genetic screening Tests performed during pregnancy to detect genetic abnormalities such as Down's syndrome or Trisomy 18 (Edward's syndrome) in the foetus.

Gestation Generally counted in weeks, the period of time a baby has been carried in the uterus (gestation is counted from the first day of the last menstrual period).

Gynaecologist (GYN) A doctor specializing in women's reproductive health.

Incompetent cervix The term for a cervix that opens before labour begins.

Induction The use of medical drugs to encourage labour to begin.

Labour The process of childbirth, from early contractions to the delivery of the baby and later the placenta.

Lactation The production of milk in the breasts that follows from childbirth.

Lamaze A method of controlling pain during childbirth through relaxation and rhythmic breathing patterns.

Lanugo The fine, downy hair that temporarily covers a foetus from 26 weeks or so until birth.

Latching on The movement in which the baby makes the correct connection to the nipple in order to breastfeed.

Linea nigra A dark, vertical line that develops on the abdomen during pregnancy.

Lochia A form of vaginal discharge and bleeding that begins after delivery and tapers off gradually over around six weeks.

Meconium The baby's greenish-brown first stool.

Moulding The temporary reshaping of a baby's head during birth, which occurs due to pressure from the birth canal and pelvic bones.

Neonatal The time from a baby's birth to 28 days after the birth.

Neural tube defect A birth defect that affects the baby's brain or spine.

Obstetrician A doctor specializing in pregnancy, labour and the postnatal period.

Oxytocin A hormone secreted by the body during birth that causes uterine contractions.

Paediatrician A doctor specializing in the medical care of infants and children.

Perinatal The time immediately before and after birth.

Perineum The area on a woman's body between the vagina and rectum.

Placenta An organ that develops in the uterus to connect the foetus to the woman's body via the umbilical cord.

Postnatal period The time period between delivery and 6–8 weeks after the birth.

Pre-eclampsia A medical condition during pregnancy characterized by high blood pressure and blood proteins; if untreated, can progress to eclampsia.

Premature baby A baby born before 37 weeks' gestation.

Premature labour Labour that occurs between 20 and 37 weeks' gestation.

Prenatal Before birth.

Show The passing of the mucus plug that sealed the cervical canal during pregnancy.

Spinal block A type of anaesthesia administered into the base of the spine once, via injection, to numb the lower body.

TENS (transcutaneous electrical nerve stimulation) A hand-held device that delivers mild bursts of electricity through the skin, which works to alleviate pain.

Transitional labour The end of the first stage of labour when the cervix dilates through strong, very fast recurring contractions.

Trimester A time period of three months; pregnancy is divided into three trimesters.

Umbilical cord A cord of tissue that connects the foetus to the placenta.

Uterus A hollow, muscular organ in which the foetus grows.

Vernix A white, creamy substance that covers the foetus during the last trimester.

Index

Acknowledgements

Author acknowledgements

Huge thanks to all you dads (and mums) who generously gave me your time, honesty and ideas. To my editor Sarah Tomley and designer Tracy Killick for your skill and (almost) never-ending patience through the writing and production process. Thanks for keeping me on my toes. To my wife Charlotte for your love, support, encouragement and insight especially when I was wandering off track. I've learned so much about being a better dad by watching you being a mum. Finally, to Jack, Finn and Will, who every day are teaching me how to be a better father. I love you dudes. You rock.

Picture credits

Incidental images used throughout.
Fotolia: Andrey7777777; Anna; Arôme; Draganm; Gstudio; HuHu Lin; Ilyaka; Log88off; Lom; Pavel Losevsky; Milan Petrovic; Tpandd
Shutterstock: Vividz Foto; W. Jarva; Osijan

Quercus Publishing Plc
55 Baker Street, 7th Floor,
South Block, London W1U 8EW

First published in 2013

Copyright © Quercus 2013

A catalogue record of this book is available from the British Library

ISBN 978 1 78206 134 2

Printed and bound in China

10 9 8 7 6 5 4 3 2 1

Produced for Quercus Publishing Plc by Tracy Killick Art Direction and Design

Commissioning editor: Sarah Tomley (of www.editorsonline.org)
Designer: Tracy Killick
Project editors: Ben Way and Alice Bowden
Proof-reader: Catherine Larner
Illustrator: Victoria Woodgate (www.vickywoodgate.com)
Indexer: Hilary Bird